THE COMPLETE
SNOWBOARDER

SECOND EDITION

THE COMPLETE
SNOWBOARDER

SECOND EDITION

JEFF BENNETT,
SCOTT DOWNEY, AND CHARLES ARNELL

RAGGED MOUNTAIN PRESS / McGraw-Hill
Camden, Maine · New York · San Francisco · Washington, D.C.
Auckland · Bogotá · Caracas · Lisbon · London · Madrid
Mexico City · Milan · Montreal · New Delhi
San Juan · Singapore · Sydney · Tokyo · Toronto

To Tonya,
for laughing at me when I really needed it!

Ragged Mountain Press
A Division of The McGraw-Hill Companies

10 9 8 7 6
Copyright © 1994, 2001 Jeff Bennett
All rights reserved. The publisher takes no responsibility for the use of any of the
materials or methods described in this book, nor for the products thereof. The name
"Ragged Mountain Press" and the Ragged Mountain Press logo are trademarks of
The McGraw-Hill Companies. Printed in the United States of America.

Library of Congress Cataloging-in-Publication Data
Bennett, Jeff, 1961-
    The complete snowboarder / Jeff Bennett, Scott Downey, and Charles Arnell.—2nd ed.
        p.   cm.
    Includes index.
    ISBN 0-07-135787-4
    1. Snowboarding. I. Downey, Scott. II. Arnell, Charles. III. Title.

    GV857.S57 B46 2000
    796.9—dc21   00-039059

Questions regarding the content of this book should be addressed to
Ragged Mountain Press
P.O. Box 220
Camden, ME 04843
www.raggedmountainpress.com

Questions regarding the ordering of this book should be addressed to
The McGraw-Hill Companies
Customer Service Department
P.O. Box 547
Blacklick, OH 43004
Retail customers: 1-800-262-4729
Bookstores: 1-800-722-4726

This book is printed on 70-lb Citation by Quebecor Printing, Fairfield, PA
Design by Gay Kempton and Shannon B. Thomas
Photography by Brian Robb or Jeff Bennett except where otherwise credited
Production management by Dan Kirchoff
Edited by Thomas McCarthy and Don Graydon

Contents

Introduction

Snow, sun, sky, and mountains: snowboarding is a great way to experience the outdoors. PHOTO OF DAN RAY BY JOHN KELLY

First tracks. The sun climbs low over my right shoulder, softening the nip of the crisp morning air. Swathed in loose layers of high-tech insulants and warm, comfortable boots, I peer down my favorite run. Last night's storm has blanketed the mountain in knee-deep powder. Snowboarder's nirvana.

With a couple of quick tugs, I'm buckled into my bindings and raring to go. I hop once to turn the board downhill and take off. In seconds I'm flowing down the fall line. Surfing the slopes. The board floats from one turn to the next, my body rising and sinking in rhythm with the turns. Total freedom. I spot a small jump to one side of the trail, hit a backside air, and stick the landing before melting back into the ride. Moments later, I slow to a relaxing glide as the mountain rolls out into the valley. In the lift line my mind drifts away, back to my first days as a snowboarder.

I followed a roundabout path to snowboarding, beginning with curious glances at my freeriding peers as I struggled to master the basics of alpine skiing. As an average skier, I found myself spending more time snapping boots back into bindings or searching for half-buried poles and goggles than I spent skiing. Nonetheless, my enthusiasm for the slopes persisted. I just needed something to keep me on them with some degree of dignity. Coming from a background of slalom waterskiing, I longed to be back on one board, yet free to carve the mountain.

Snowboarding appeared to be a natural extension of my prior experiences. A sport that would combine my semicoordinated athletic capabilities with my passion for winter and snow. So I peppered the local boardheads with questions, watched the latest videos, and waited for this inane wave of curiosity to fade. It didn't.

My curiosity hit a euphoric peak when I found myself driving toward my favorite ski area. From the comfort of my pickup's passenger compartment, my imagination reeled. I envisioned moments of weightless ecstasy, doing 180- and 360-degree spins off car-sized bumps, and carving giant, arcing turns through fresh powder.

I stepped into the resort's board shop, plunked down some money, and rented my first snowboard. Within minutes I found myself standing atop a fitting platform, answering probing questions about my personality ("Are you regular or goofy?"), and staring down upon the alien contraption that would eventually provide countless hours of entertainment. The friendly technician scampering about my feet made some final adjustments to the bindings, offered some kind words of advice and encouragement, and sent me on my way.

Marching out the lodge's back door, I calmly strode to the top of the easiest slope I could find and anxiously buckled my boots into the bindings. "All right . . . my first snowboarding adventure!" my mind exclaimed. "Here goes!"

It took precisely two seconds from the moment I started sliding to realize that I had no clue how to control my snowboard. I stood up, I sat down. I slid a few feet, I fell. A few more feet, and I spun backward. I managed to make it to the bottom of the slope, snow-covered but smiling. Once there, I made a decision: "Rather than spend my day rolling through the snow like some circus tumbler, I'll take an introductory snowboarding class."

Under the patient guidance of a seasoned snowboarding instructor, I learned how to walk around with my board, how to get off a chairlift, and how to make skidded turns without splatting. By the end of the first day, I'd fallen dozens of times and had barely acquired enough skills to call myself a novice snowboarder, but I was hooked!

Today I look back upon my early misadventures with incredible fondness, for they opened the door to a world of fun and challenges. At the same time, I wish that I'd purchased a thick, durable butt pad early on or found a comprehensive book that would have quickly guided me through snowboarding's fundamental theories and techniques. Although I continued to avail myself of professional instruction, I found many skills evolving after my snowboarding lessons ended. I spent a lot of time blundering down slopes, wondering why my board wasn't going where I wanted it to, only to find out that just one tip from an instructor could cure a whole day's worth of trials and errors.

This second edition of The Complete Snowboarder takes you down the same snow-covered paths that I traveled before, and still travel today. If you have never been on a snowboard before, this book will convey the essence of snowboarding and help you decide whether you'd like to try it. If you are an experienced beginner, it will help you refine and improve your techniques. Finally, advanced snowboarders will find the latest information on snowboarding's hottest endeavors—freestyle, halfpipe riding, alpine riding, and racing. Throughout the book, top pros provide valuable advice on the ins and outs of snowboarding and keep you progressing by leaps and bounds. The second edition has updated techniques, expanded coverage of backcountry snowboarding, and new equipment updates from boots and body gear to bindings and board designs.

From the history of snowboarding to snowboarding equipment; from turning techniques to ski area etiquette; and from advanced terrain tactics to the competitive challenges available to the most die-hard boarders, The Complete Snowboarder is a full course, with everything you need to know to enjoy the exciting sport of snowboarding.

About the Authors

When I finally decided to try snowboarding, I realized I'd discovered a sport that I could do without inflicting unnecessary harm to my ego. Snowboarding drew upon a slightly different set of skills than those used in skiing—skills that even I possessed. At the same time, I realized that I needed the advice and expertise of someone who could make sense of this mystifying sport. For this second edition, Scott Downey and Charles Arnell were those experts.

It takes little more than a quick glance through snowboarding magazines, Sims videos, or Warren Miller movies to tell that Scott Downey has been riding the leading edge of snowboarding for many years. As a member of the Sims World Cup Team, he tallied many top-10 finishes on the U.S. Pro Tours and World Cup Series. At the 1987 Breckenridge World Cup, Scott forever changed halfpipe riding by designing the first in-the-ground halfpipe with roll-out style skateboard decks. Not one to rest on his laurels, Scott went on to create Sorel's Pro-Flex snowboarding boots and Thorlo's snowboard socks. Scott now coaches tomorrow's pros as the head freestyle coach for High Cascade Snowboard Camp and acts as the Snowboarding Ambassador for Mount Bachelor near his home in Bend, Oregon.

Charles Arnell has been snowboarding since the mid 1980s, and has logged well over 1,000 days on the snow. He was one of the first PSIA-certified snowboarding instructors and has taught hundreds of snowboarders at resorts from Vail, Colorado, to Mount Hutt, New Zealand. Charles turned pro in 1989 and earned several top-10 finishes in snowboarding events around the world. He founded the Mt. Hood Summer Snowboard Camp after his first few years of professional competition and was its director until 1996. He started Arnell Snowboards in 1993 and later became president of Snowboard Systems Inc., a snowboarding technology development company.

Scott, Charles, and I joined heads for this book. We combine the skills of riders and writers. While Scott and Charles link turns on the back bowls of your favorite mountains, I will link their snowboarding knowledge with user-friendly prose. While they're out there making things look easy, I'll make all of the typical beginner mistakes. As you and I head down the slopes, you can laugh at me, learn from Scott and Charles, and enjoy yourself all at the same time.

As an extra bonus, a handful of the world's hottest snowboarders and snowboard instructors have pitched in to make this book the best of its kind. Handy sidebars by John Calkins, Mike Estes, Matt Goodwill, Lowell Hart, Mike Jacoby, Craig Kelly, Hillary Maybery, J. D. Platt, Jimi Scott, and David Sher dial you into the nuances of snowboarding, making each lesson more fruitful and rewarding.

A Little Help from Our Friends

I value my unique position as author of the second edition of *The Complete Snowboarder*, for I am sharing a hillside seat with you. We will both learn from snowboarding's best teachers, their words captured in this book so that we can come back to read them time and time again. The book may bear my name, but I am only a mediator between the pros and you, the student.

David Sher deserves much of the credit for this book. David is owner of Mountain and Surf Pro Shop in Sacramento, California, the 1991 California State Overall All Around Master's Snowboarding Champion, and the founder of Billiard Snowboard Products. It was he who got this book off the ground, kept us inspired, and nurtured the book from dream to reality.

I would like to thank Ken Achenback, Paul Alden, Lonnie Ball, Cecilia Boettcher, Scott Clum, Jackie DiFilippo, John Fry, Rich Dusablon, Shane Glasgow, Jimmy Halopoff, Sharon Harned, Ken Hermer, J. P. Ingersoll, Ken Kelly, Kevin Kinnear, Matt Kennedy, Craig Kiefel, Roger Lohr, Dave Margolis, Ted Martin, Bruce Maurey, Dorcas Miller, Rob Morrow, Gaylene Nagel, Katherine O'Melchuck, John Packer, Doug Palladini, Mike Paulino, Shawn Peterson, Geoff Potter, Steve Rechtschaffner, John Rice, Kathleen Ring, Lee Rogers, Keith Scott, Brian Selstrom, Mike Shaw, Sean Sullivan, Allison Thompson, John Tullis, Randy Walters, Travis Yamada, and Kirk Zack for their support and contributions.

Thanks also to the many publications, manufacturers, shops, and resorts for contributing their resources to this book: Blackcomb, Blast, Burton Snowboards, Copper Mountain, Snowboard Core, Eastern Edge, Extreme Comp Ski and Sport, John Fry, Heine Pipe Tools, High Cascade Snowboard Camp, Hot Snowboards, IMI Designs, Ltd., Industrial Strength Communications, International Snowboard Federation, Kemper Snowboards, Lamar Snowboards, Luxury Snowboards, Morrow Snowboards, Mt. Bachelor Ski and Summer Resort, Montana Powder Guides, Mountain and Surf Pro Shop, National Ski Areas Association, Nitro Snowboards, Professional Ski Instructors of America, Progressive Images, Sims Snowboards, Ski Industries of America, Snow Summit, *Snowboarder* magazine, The Snoboard Shop, Sorel, Stowe Mountain Resort, Timberline Ski Area, Transworld Snowboarding, United States Forest Service, USSA, Warp, and Yakima.

What Are You Getting Yourself Into?

If you have any friends who snowboard, you already know how addictive the sport can be. In its purest form, snowboarding provides a sensational link between you and nature. The board glides over a frictionless surface of snow crystals, pulled downhill by the forces of gravity. All you have to do is to learn how these forces work and use them to your own enjoyment. At its extreme, snowboarding is wild and untamed—a world of acrobatics that springs from the minds of spirited riders and recoils just in time to stick a perfect landing.

In many ways, learning to snowboard will be no different from learning to ride a skateboard or a surfboard—only easier! It will take you a day or two to get the feel for sliding on snow, but once you pass through the comedy of errors that befall every novice, an exhilarating revelation will emerge. You will discover that snowboarding can be learned faster than any other downhill pursuit. There will be no skis to cross, no poles to plant, and only one edge to deal with at a time.

If you give it your best, you can acquire enough skills in your first two or three days of snowboard-

ing to comfortably carry you from beginner slopes to intermediate runs. Then, as your confidence and ability grow, those same basic skills will guide you down more challenging runs with only slight modifications.

Ultimately, snowboarding will become whatever you make of it. Your board can launch you high above the lips of your favorite halfpipe, or provide a tool to bring you back in touch with the natural splendor of winter. With snowboarding meaning so many things to so many people, you will always have a fantastic array of snowboarding opportunities, from your choice of equipment to the type of terrain you ride. Snowboarding is also a matter of style, and boarders develop their style in different ways. Every move you make will be your own, each adding a unique twist to the sport.

Is Snowboarding for You?

If you are physically fit, possess average coordination, and feel that you could ski (whether you have ever skied or not), it is likely that you have what it takes to be a snowboarder. You can be middle-aged or teenaged, a skateboarder or a ski racer, a full-time athlete or a weekend warrior. No matter what your background, snowboarding offers new ways to enjoy the slopes. You don't have to set your sights on riding steep bowls, moguls, or halfpipes. Instead, snowboarding could be your opportunity to simply spend days gliding through linked turns, to feel the crisp air against your face and absorb the sensation of your board floating from one turn into another.

Those of you who do come from a background of skiing, skateboarding, or surfing are probably already used to balancing on a slippery surface. If you've done well in those sports, chances are that the skills you already possess will transfer into snowboarding naturally. Skiing will help you understand concepts like edging, carving, and unweighting; freestyle riding will feel like skateboarding on snow; and huge turns in deep powder will remind surfers of giant bottom turns. Plus, the physical coordination, mettle, and attitude you've acquired in these other sports will make your first days on a snowboard more enjoyable.

Remember, snowboarding is a sport with something for everyone!

Snowboarding History

At first glance, snowboarding bears striking similarities to skiing, surfing, and skateboarding. Although snowboarding has been influenced by all three, modern snowboarding attributes its origins to Sherman Poppin's Snurfer. The Snurfer first appeared in the 1960s and looked like a cross between a plywood sled and a skateboard deck. A handheld rope was attached to the nose of the board to give its rider something to hold onto, and steel tacks poked through the upper deck to hold the rider's feet in place.

Snurfer riders were brave souls, for the board offered little—if any—directional control. It was a remarkably crazy toy, specially suited for those with nerves of steel and bones of rubber.

As snowboarding glided into the early 1980s,

An early Sims snowboard at Mammoth, California, circa 1977. PHOTO OF LONNIE TOFT BY TOM SIMS, COURTESY SIMS SNOWBOARDS

technological advances accumulated, and the modern snowboard began to emerge. Legendary figures like Tom Sims and Jake Burton Carpenter pioneered the way for modern boards by incorporating ski technology—P-Tex bases, steel edges, wood and fiberglass composites—into their snowboards. Demetre Malovich likewise made some big snowboard performance inroads: by integrating sidecut, swallowtails, and sandwich construction, he created the celebrated Winterstick board.

As the grand patriarchs of the sport refined and improved their snowboards, other advances appeared. Jeff Grell designed the first highback binding, finally making it possible to control snowboards on hard-packed snow, and Burton Snowboards introduced the first version of today's soft boot.

Advances in snowboarding equipment had some welcome side effects. These technological advances gave the sport respect and opened the doors to snowboarding throughout the world. It's hard to believe, looking at the number of snowboarders today, that only 39 of approximately 600 ski areas allowed snowboarding in 1985! Today, snowboarding is allowed just about everywhere thanks to the hard work and determination of the sport's founders.

How to Use This Book

This book is arranged in a simple, user-friendly format that takes you from the floor of your local board shop to the slopes at your favorite ski resort. As you progress through each stage of snowboarding, you will move farther up the hill, testing your newfound skills as you go. If you have never ridden a snowboard before, start with page 1 and keep reading. As you progress from chapter to chapter, you will learn new concepts and acquire new skills that will carry into future chapters. After a day at the mountain, come back to where you left off, read some more, then go ride again. More experienced boarders can jump to later chapters and pick up the information they need to break through learning plateaus or learn new tricks.

Though this book teaches snowboarding with descriptions and diagrams, it is ultimately just a book—little more than a collection of frozen glimpses at a fluid sport. The techniques taught here

TIPS FOR CROSSOVER SKIERS

Once you're comfortable skiing anything on the mountain, it can challenge your ego to head back to the bunny slopes to learn how to snowboard. If you're a first-time snowboarder coming from a background of skiing, bring your skis to the mountain and just snowboard for half a day. That way you can get the high-speed adrenaline rush you're used to, and learn to snowboard—all in the same day.

There's a catch though. Once you try snowboarding, you may never want to get back on skis!

—Scott Downey

work best when you have a competent snowboard instructor to demonstrate and coach you through each maneuver. I highly recommend that you seek instruction early in your snowboarding career, and that you revisit a professional instructor periodically to refine your snowboarding techniques.

Keep in mind that snowboarding is a sport of incredible variety—from the types of equipment used by different snowboarders, to the types of stances boarders choose. This variety carries with it a multitude of techniques, each suited to a particular style of riding. This book cuts a broad swath through the middle of the technique jungle, leaving new riders with enough how-to information to invent their own riding style.

In the end, this book will exercise the most important part of your body: your brain. Through imagery and explanation, the second edition of *The Complete Snowboarder* will give you the mental tools you need to get down the slope. With the time you spend on the slopes—learning by both mistake and triumph—you will advance faster and more efficiently than you had ever dreamed possible.

1 Getting Started
A Snowboarding Primer

Jonny Beall, Wishbone Images

You've seen snowboards on the slopes, in your favorite magazines, and on television as an Olympic sport. Now how do *you* find a snowboard and learn to ride it?

One of the cheapest ways to break into snowboarding is to befriend someone with a spare board and enough patience to guide you through the basic learning stages. However, if you have a few bucks to spare, your first snowboard should be rented from a snowboard shop, and your first trip down the slopes should be under the watchful eye of a professional instructor. The tips you pick up from a pro will help you have fun and learn fast. Plus, your friends will appreciate not having to listen to a barrage of questions as you waddle through your first attempts at boarding.

Snowboard rentals and instruction are available at almost every ski area. In fact, most places that offer ski instruction offer beginner courses in snowboarding too. Call around to a few of your favorite ski areas and see what types of programs they offer beginners. With a little investigation, you may be able to find

Snowboarding instructors can make your first few days on the slopes more rewarding and enjoyable. JACK AFFLECK, COURTESY VAIL ASSOCIATES

inexpensive first-timer packages that include equipment rental, a lift ticket, and an introductory course in snowboarding.

If you rent a snowboard, but choose not to seek professional instruction, you can still learn to ride. You'll progress a little more slowly and may fall a few more times, but this book will guide you through the learning stages so you can begin snowboarding on your own. Start on a bunny hill, take it slow, and learn the basics. Then you can ask more experienced snowboarders to critique your riding and give you some pointers.

Whatever you do, don't plunk down a lot of money for new equipment before your first couple of days have passed. Though you're likely to discover the joys of snowboarding fast and will want to buy your own equipment, the first few days will let you test the waters. Then if you decide you want your own equipment, the tips you've picked up in those first days will make it easier to find gear that's right for you.

RENTING A SNOWBOARD

Want to get a big jump on your first day of snowboarding? Rent your snowboard the day before your first lesson. That way you can take it home and strap it on in your living room. Try rocking onto the edges, hopping, or swiveling the board. By the time you actually hit the slopes, you'll already have a feel for the snowboard and you'll be a lot more comfortable. By the way, do this on an old rug or blanket, and don't try this with a freshly waxed board. Also, move the furniture or you'll spend more time fixing your living room than learning to snowboard!

—David Sher,
Mountain and Surf Pro Shop,
Sacramento, California

Snowboard shops are a great place to explore your equipment options and to ask questions about snowboarding. COURTESY EXTREME COMP, PORTLAND, OREGON

Elements of Style: Snowboarding Equipment

Few winter sports offer more freedom than snowboarding. All you really need is a board, boots, and some essential accessories. In the few minutes it takes to put them all together, you can be ready to hit the mountain.

In this section, we'll take a look at the equipment you'll be using on the slopes. We'll talk about different types of snowboards, bindings, and boots. The names and lingo you pick up here will get you ready for the riding instructions you'll read about later.

What's a Snowboard?

Let's start by taking a look at a typical snowboard—one quite similar to the snowboards you're bound to see on the slopes today. By examining the board and learning the names for its parts, you

will find it easier to understand techniques discussed later.

Take a look at any of the snowboards in this book. They look a bit like short, fat skis, don't they? Well, that shouldn't come as much of a surprise. Modern snowboard designs are deeply rooted in alpine ski technology, borrowing everything from shapes to materials. And, ironically, snowboarding technology is now changing the sport of skiing as ski manufacturers make radical changes to incorporate snowboard designs. In fact, today's shaped skis are really just long, skinny snowboards. So if you are familiar with alpine skis, you'll find that the terms used to describe snowboard components are pretty much the same as those used for skis.

If you have never been around snowboards before, take a moment to study the accompanying diagram, then read the description of each part. If you've got a snowboard handy, find each part on it yourself. Learn to tell the tip from the tail, and

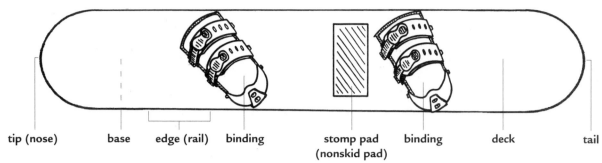

tip (nose)   base   edge (rail)   binding   stomp pad   binding   deck   tail
                                                    (nonskid pad)

Parts of a snowboard

the deck from the base. That way, when we start talking about things like bindings, edges, or stomp pads, you'll be able to keep up.

Tip (Nose)

The nose is the front of your board. There, that was an easy start to board anatomy, wasn't it? Well, what if both ends of your board look the same? Check out the graphics on the board: these should give you some clues. Also, look to see if one end is turned up higher than the other. The higher end will usually be the tip. Finally, if your board is designed for alpine riding or racing, the tip may be more pointy than the tail.

Tail

The tail is the back of the board. In some boards, the tail is flatter and more square-cut than the tip. However, some boards—known as *twin tips*—have an identical, symmetrical tip and tail. A twin-tip snowboard, shaped the same at both ends, is typically designed for freestyle use. The tip is determined by the direction of the graphics: turn the board on its side, read any words printed on it, and the tip is to the left of the written words when they are right-side up. And once you know which end is the tip, you've got a pretty good clue about which end is the tail.

Deck

This is the protective top-sheet of the board, and the place where the bindings are mounted. To make sure the bindings stay firmly mounted, most snowboards have threaded inserts—mounting holes built right into the deck—that accept matching bolts. All you do is bolt the binding into the inserts in much the same way bolts are screwed into nuts. To change the position of the bindings, just unscrew the bolts, reposition the bindings, and put the bolts in the matching set of inserts. This system is a big plus for beginners who are still experimenting with different stances, making changes easy. However, the number of binding positions is limited by the number and configuration of the inserts.

Base

The base is simply the bottom of the board. Bases are almost always made out of a tough polyethylene known as *P-Tex*. P-Tex bases can be *extruded* (melted and pushed through a narrow slot, then cut to shape) or *sintered* (ground into a fine powder, then pressed, heated, and sliced to shape).

Extruded bases are inexpensive to manufacture, but do not hold as much wax as many sintered bases. Extruded bases do, however, retain wax for a long time. Sintered bases are more expensive to manufacture and, being more porous, have a higher wax capacity. If you're searching for speed, sintered bases are the way to go. They'll run faster and glide better if you diligently wax and maintain them.

Graphite base materials are one step in quality above sintered P-Tex bases. Graphite bases are made with higher-molecular-weight plastics designed to hold wax better, and they often provide faster running surfaces than sintered P-Tex bases. Graphite bases typically appear on high-performance racing boards and, more recently, on high-end freestyle boards. Since graphite bases only come in a deep, dark black, they are easy to spot in the store and on the hill.

Edge (Rail)

The edge is where the base meets the board's sidewalls. Edges are narrow strips of steel that run from tip to tail. When the board is tilted, the metal edges slice through the snow, helping the board grip and carve through turns. Even if the edge wraps all the way around the board, snowboarders talk in terms of two edges: the *toe edge* and the *heel edge*. When you stand on your snowboard, the toe edge is the edge closest to your toes, and the heel edge is the edge closest to your heels.

Stomp Pad (Nonskid Pad)

This is a rubber or soft plastic mat that sticks to the top of the deck between the bindings. It keeps your back foot on the board when it isn't locked into the back binding—like when you're getting off a chairlift or skating across a flat area. Without a stomp pad, your back foot could slip off the board, catch the ground, and pull your legs apart. (Don't test this on your own, just get a stomp pad!)

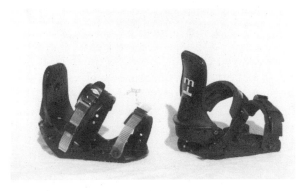

Highback bindings clamp soft boots to the snowboard with two or three buckled straps. BINDINGS COURTESY SIMS AND MORROW

Bindings

Think of bindings as boot harnesses and you'll have a perfect concept of their intended purpose. Bindings fasten your boots to the snowboard, making you and your snowboard one unit.

There are three major types of snowboard bindings: *highback (soft) bindings*, *step-in bindings*, and *plate bindings*. The type you choose depends on the type of boot you're using, and vice versa.

Highback (Soft) Bindings

These are plastic contraptions that clamp soft boots (more on those later) to the board with two or three buckled straps. Basically the boot fits in a contoured base plate and is held there by the straps. These straps, in turn, are held tight by ratchets that grab serrations in the straps themselves. While the straps hold your feet down, a vertical plastic plate—called a highback—rises behind your ankles and lower calves. The full system gives you great contact with your board, which translates into control when you are riding.

The main variations in highback bindings are the height and shape of the highback and the number and flexibility of the straps. Your local shop rep can help you select the binding that matches your board and the type of riding you'll be doing.

Alpine snowboarders and aggressive freeriders (folks who spend most of their time carving turns rather than doing tricks) favor taller, stiffer, more cup-shaped highbacks. This gives them greater contact with the board and can improve edge control—especially on the heel edge.

Halfpipe enthusiasts and freestylers, on the other hand (folks who go for a lot of ground and air tricks), need plenty of lower leg motion, so they tend toward shorter, lower highbacks. The freestyle highback stays out of the way of their legs, making it easier to twist and tweak during tricks.

Step-In Bindings

These bindings were introduced to snowboarding as an alternative to strap bindings, mainly to provide a more convenient method of engaging the

Step-in bindings *can make it easier to get into and get out of your bindings.*

foot to the snowboard. Many of the early designs used what is commonly referred to as a soft step-in boot, or a hybrid boot. These early designs were typically stiffer than a traditional soft boot and required a stiff center shank to help them stay in place. Therefore some performance and comfort were lost for the sake of easy entry.

More recently, some advanced step-in boot and binding technologies have incorporated true soft boots with step-in capabilities, making this the system of choice for many snowboarders.

Plate Bindings

Plate bindings are low-profile mouse traps that lock hard boots (more on those later, too) securely to the board. Plate bindings consist of a sturdy base plate, burly steel bails, and a heel or toe lever. When the boot is inserted in the binding, the bails reach

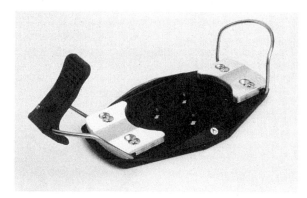

Plate bindings *lock hard boots securely to the snowboard.*
COURTESY BURTON SNOWBOARDS

WHY DO I NEED TO WEAR A LEASH?

Most ski areas were built with skiers in mind—not snowboarders. Long, flat traverses don't faze skiers, because they can pole and skate their way across the flats. Snowboarders, on the other hand, have to skate with their back foot off the board or carry the board over to a steeper hill. The leash should always be attached to your leg when you're walking or skating. If you're carrying your snowboard, loop the strap around your wrist so the board can't get away and become a dangerous missile.

—Scott Downey

up and grab the boot's heel and toe protrusions. To lock the bails in place, you just flip the heel or toe lever upward and you're ready to go. Plate bindings are favored by racers and hard-carving freeriders when precise edge control is desired.

Ultimately you can try out all types of bindings and ride whatever boot and binding combination you like best. When you ride different types of bindings, snowboarding feels like many sports in one.

Leash

The leash straps your front leg to the front binding with a short length of cord or webbing. Should your board ever desire to tour the slopes without you, the leash keeps it from straying very far. Leashes also keep resort owners happy since leashes are required everywhere you go.

Boots

Specially designed snowboarding boots significantly improve the quality of your boarding experience. They protect your feet and ankles from the rigors of high-speed turns and arch-busting straps, keep your feet toasty on the coldest days, and help

Hybrid step-in boots combine soft-boot technology with step-in binding technology. COURTESY SNOWJAM BOOTS

achieve a proper fit between your feet and your bindings. There are three main varieties: *soft boots*, *hard boots*, and *hybrid step-in boots*.

Soft Boots

A soft boot has two parts—an inner bladder and an outer boot. The inner bladder is thick and sturdy, very much like a ski-boot bladder. The bladders keep your feet warm and dry, and they put some padding between your feet and the bindings. The outer boot has a soft, flexible upper that allows plenty of ankle movement, and a deeply treaded sole that seats firmly in the base of highback bindings.

Soft boots (and soft-boot step-ins) attract freestylers, free-riders, and anyone looking for comfort or increased flexibility. They also attract some crossover skiers who want to be able to drive to and from the slopes in their snowboard boots.

Hard Boots

For total edge control, many snowboarders lean toward a stiffer boot, the hard boot. If you didn't know any better, you could easily mistake hard boots for skiing or mountaineering boots. Hard boots have sturdy plastic shells that close around a thick inner boot with buckles or ratchet bails. Hinges are often built into the ankles to recover some forward flex without sacrificing performance. In addition to having stiffer uppers than most soft boots, hard boots have stiffer soles to ensure that they will anchor firmly into plate bindings without danger of bending and popping free.

The stiffness of hard boots transfers body movements directly through the plate bindings and into the board. This provides greater control when carving high-speed turns, making hard boots a favorite of racers, alpine riders, and crossover skiers who want to retain that alpine skiing feel.

Hybrid Step-In Boots

Hybrids are soft boots that incorporate step-in binding technology. These soft boots feel much like the traditional soft boots used with strap systems, minus the inconvenience of straps. Many freeriders and freestylers claim the soft-boot step-in designs outperform standard soft boots.

Hard boots have sturdy, plastic outer shells that close around a thick inner boot with buckles or ratchet bails. They are used together with plate bindings.

SNOWBOARD BOOTS

Indulge yourself when buying snowboard boots: they can make or break your day, depending on whether they keep your feet warm and comfortable. Pick a pair that feels a little snug at first, without cutting off your circulation. Eventually the boot's inner bladder will compress, and the boot will fit you perfectly. Next, make sure that your heels anchor firmly into the bottom of the boot. Heel lift makes it a lot tougher to tilt your snowboard onto its toeside edge. If you already own a pair of soft boots and you're having trouble keeping your heels down, try using a *heel anchor*—a three-way strap that pulls the boot in tight around your foot to keep your heel in place.

—David Sher, Mountain and Surf Pro Shop, Sacramento, California

Hybrid step-in boots combine hard soles with soft, flexible uppers. Though not as comfortable as traditional soft boots, the hybrids give riders the stiff sole and some of the control that comes from a hard boot, while retaining much of the flexibility of the upper of a soft boot. This stiffer feel for the board, compared with the standard soft boot, makes the hybrids a favorite with some alpine riders and snowboarders crossing over from skiing.

Let's Go Shopping: Selecting Your Snowboard

Now that you know a bit about snowboards, how do you know which board is right for you? Pro riders have boards built to their specifications—boards that combine just the right amount of sidecut, flex, camber, and length for their body weight and riding style. All you have to do is find a pro your size who rides the way you want to ride, and you'll have the right board. Right? Wrong!

There's actually a myriad of subtle design variations that make one board quite different from another, and one board better for you than another. When you can ride most any intermediate slope without the nagging fear of splatting, you'll be able to tell which boards work best for you. But for now, just think about two things: your ideal board length and your preferred riding style.

Types of Snowboards

Riding styles have names in snowboarding—*freestyle, freeriding, alpine riding,* and *racing* cover most of the spectrum. Manufacturers recognize these divisions in riding styles by building boards to match them. Here's a look at the main categories of snowboards and a brief description of each one.

Freestyle Boards

Freestyle riders spend most of their time in halfpipes, sliding rails, jumping gaps, spinning, and bonking off anything a snowboard park has to offer. Their boards are wide and flexible, with very little camber or swing weight.

There are two main types of freestyle snowboards: *halfpipe boards* and *slopestyle boards*. A halfpipe board flexes with the curves of the pipe, yet holds an edge as it rides toward the far wall. Slopestyle boards are built wide, flat, and ultrasoft to make skateboard-style ground tricks easier to execute.

Freeriding Boards

Freeriding combines a little bit of everything, from freestyle riding to BoarderCross to alpine riding. Freeriders may be carving groomed trails one moment, riding untracked powder the next, and tossing in some freestyle tricks along the way.

Though you can freeride on any snowboard, the ones designed to be freeriding boards strike a happy medium between freestyle and alpine-racing designs. They combine characteristics of both in a one-board-fits-all program. Some freeriding boards have the stiffer characteristics of alpine boards, while others offer flexibility that more closely resembles freestyle boards.

Alpine-Racing Boards

Alpine and racing boards tend to be stiffer and stronger than freestyle or freeriding boards. They're designed to hold an edge and resist chattering when carving high-speed turns or when loaded with lots of pressure during extreme descents. Racing boards are narrow and fast and are built to hold an edge at high speed. Alpine boards share these characteristics, but are often a little sturdier in order to survive the rigors of tough mountain riding.

Keep in mind that snowboarding changes every year. Categories change, names change, and riding styles change. No matter what the riding styles are called in your area, understanding the differences between snowboards will help you select one that suits your way of riding. If you can't decide what type of board you want, just get a freeriding design and go snowboarding! In time, you'll figure out what type will be best for you.

Length

Measure your snowboard from the tip of the tip to the end of the tail and you'll have the board's length. Most boards are measured in centimeters, not inches, and generally range from 130 to 175 centimeters.

If you're renting a snowboard for the first time, the shop technician will help you select a user-friendly board length. Your correct board length is a function of your height, weight, and ability, and your intended use. Many of the snowboard brands have gender-specific models too. Some beginners have good luck picking a board that touches between their chin and nose when they stand next to it. Once you get better, you'll be able to pick just the right length for the type of riding you do: shorter boards for freestyle, longer boards for alpine riding or riding powder.

Design Techno-Talk

Pretty soon you'll be on the mountain, having fun snowboarding, and improving your skills daily. Your legs and feet will be dialed into your snowboard and more sensitive to the way your equipment performs. About the same time, you'll probably be ready to upgrade your equipment. That's when this section will come in handy by helping you pick out boards that match your style of riding. (Until then, this stuff may be just techno-garble—information that will help you talk like a shop rep. If it doesn't pique your curiosity, just flip to the next section on setting up your board.)

Many things affect the way your board performs: its *length, effective edge, tip and tail kicks, swing weight, sidecut, core construction, flex, camber,* and *torsional stiffness*. It's how these factors work together—not how they act individually—that affects the feel and performance of your snowboard. Still, let's look here at each feature individually. (See the preceding section for information on length.)

Effective Edge

Stand on your board and look at the rise, or *kick*, in the tip and tail shovels. Subtract these lengths from the board's overall length and you'll have the effective edge. In other words, the effective edge is simply the length of the edge that is actually touching the snow.

Once you figure out your ideal board length, the board with the longer effective edge will grip the snow better. When matched properly with the snowboard's overall design, this translates into better control.

Tip and Tail Kicks

Tips and tails are lifted off the snow—they have a kick—to help the board float to the top. The shape and size of the tip and tail shovels are determined by the board's intended use.

Racing boards are designed to go downhill with as much speed and control as possible. Accordingly, most of the tail kick is eliminated so that there is a lot of effective edge gripping the snow. Freestyle riders, on the other hand, spend a fair amount of time riding backward (snowboarders call this riding *switch stance* or *fakie*). Therefore, freestyle boards often have just as much kick in the tail as they do in the tip. Freeriding boards also

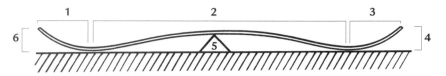

Many aspects of snowboard design affect the way your board performs. This drawing is exaggerated to show six common design elements: (1) tail shovel; (2) effective edge or run- *ning length; (3) tip shovel; (4) tip kick; (5) camber; and (6) tail kick.*

have some kick in the tail, but their kick pattern falls somewhere between racing and freestyle boards.

Swing Weight

The length of the effective edge and the amount of kick lead into a more subtle design feature called swing weight. Swing weight is a vague term that describes how much force it takes to rotate the board in the air.

Basically, here's how it works: Everything else being equal, longer boards have more weight out past your feet. That makes them harder to spin in the air than shorter boards. Here's another way to look at it: If you were to compare two boards with identical effective edges, the longer board would have more swing weight. Though both boards might feel the same on the snow, the shorter board will feel lighter in the air.

Sidecut

Lay your board flat on the floor, then turn it up on its side. You'll notice that the tip and tail are wider than the waist (center) of the board, leaving a long, arc-shaped gap between the narrowest part of the board and the floor. That arc—which gives snowboards a slight hourglass shape—is called sidecut. When your board flexes during a turn, the sidecut comes in contact with the hill and helps you carve turns.

The basic rule is that the deeper the sidecut, the sharper and smaller your comfortable turning radius. (However, the snowboard's flex, camber, and width can also affect the way the board turns.)

To understand how sidecut affects turning radius, let's use an imaginary snowboard with an ef-

fective edge of 119 centimeters and a moderate sidecut. By continuing the arc of the sidecut out from the snowboard until the arc forms a complete circle, we discover that the circle has a radius of 8 meters. This is the comfortable turning radius for that sidecut. A board with an even deeper sidecut (and therefore a smaller turning radius) would turn more sharply. A board with a shallower sidecut (and therefore a larger turning radius) wouldn't turn as sharply, but would be able to travel straighter down a hill.

As you explore the science behind sidecuts, you will find many variations. The one described above is a *radial sidecut*. If a snowboard is designed with a large-radius sidecut followed by a smaller-radius sidecut near the waist, it has a *progressive radial sidecut*. Yet another type—the *quadratic sidecut*—is shallower at its ends. The quadratic sidecut works together with the board's natural flex—which is stiffest near the board's center—to achieve a natural arc when the board is turning on the slopes.

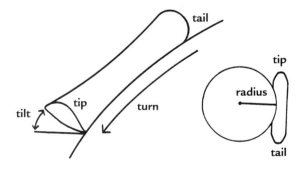

When your snowboard flexes during a turn, the sidecut comes into contact with the hill and helps you carve turns. The radius of a circle is used to measure the semicircular shape that the sidecut gives each edge of your snowboard: the smaller the radius, the tighter your snowboard can comfortably turn.

Core Construction

The core—the inside of the board—helps determine how a board feels and responds when ridden. Most snowboards have a laminated wood or polyurethane foam core, though some boards use high-tech aluminum honeycomb cores or other space-age materials. In turn these cores are surrounded with materials such as fiberglass, rubber, graphite, and Kevlar. Each manufacturer may build the core slightly different from other manufacturers as well as change the core makeup to achieve different flex and twist patterns in their snowboards.

Flex

Flex is a measure of how soft or hard a board feels when you try to bend it along its length. Stiffer boards (which usually have thicker cores) take more force to flex. However, once they're flexed, they usually grip the snow better and are more stable due to the greater force driving through them. For that reason, racers, aggressive freeriders, and heavier riders often lean toward stiffer boards. Softer-flexing boards (which usually have thinner cores) are ideal for lighter or less aggressive riders and excel in performing freestyle tricks.

Camber

Unless you're standing on your board, the center of the board's base will be permanently bowed off the ground. This bridge-like arc is called camber. Camber transfers your weight to the entire edge—not just to the center of the board. This helps the board carve and grip the snow better during turns. Camber can also act as a spring, propelling the board from one turn to another.

Torsional Stiffness

Torsional stiffness is a measure of how hard it is to twist the board along its length. Torsionally stiff boards grip the snow better and chatter less at high speeds, but they can be less forgiving. Boards with softer torsional stiffness, on the other hand, tend to be more forgiving, but have less edge grip. As with flex, alpine riders and racers lean toward stiffer boards, while freestylers tend to favor softer boards.

New technologies are being used to control torsional stiffness. Some incorporate carbon fiber stiffeners, while others harness the natural static electricity created when a snowboard speeds across the snow. Manufacturers are constantly devising innovations to increase the performance of their snowboards.

Putting It Together: Setting Up Your Board
Regular and Goofy Stances

Boarders stand sideways across their boards, one foot in front of the other. This raises an interesting question: which foot goes in front? Whether you're renting or borrowing your snowboard, *now* is the time to figure this out, since once you start learning in one stance it can be difficult and discouraging to switch.

Long before snowboards existed, surfers invented names for the way you stand. If you ride with your left foot forward you are a *regular foot*; if you ride with your right foot forward you are a *goofy foot*. (Goofy doesn't have anything to do with personality quirks!) "Yeah," you're saying, "but I've never been on a snowboard before. How should I know which foot I want forward?"

Have you ever ridden a skateboard, slalom water ski, or surfboard? If you have, use the same stance you used before. If you answered no to all three, these tests might work for you:

- Use the same stance you would use to bat or throw a baseball.
- Pretend you're running across an icy pond and that you're going to slide. Which foot would you lead with? That may be your front foot.
- Lie on your stomach like you're going to do a push-up. Now, jump up and land with one foot forward. Snowboard the way you land.

Snowboarders stand sideways on their boards. If your left foot is forward, you are **regular***.*
If you're **goofy***, you ride with your right foot forward.*

- Pretend you're running up to kick a ball. Which foot do you plant, and which do you kick with? Try putting the kicking foot in the back binding.
- Lead with the same foot you would lead with if you were doing a cartwheel.
- If all else fails, remember one important fact: 80 percent of all snowboarders are regular foot. There is only a 20 percent chance that you are goofy foot!

None of these tests are goof-proof. It may take getting on a snowboard before you'll be able to tell whether you're regular or goofy. If you can try both stances on a pair of snowboards, select the stance that feels most comfortable. On your first day of snowboarding, you may feel like you put the wrong foot forward. This feeling can be caused by placing your weight on your rear foot, causing that foot to be pulled down the hill first. If you choose a particular stance direction, stay with it for at least a couple of runs. Then if you feel you aren't progressing at the rate you should, try the opposite stance.

Stance Width

The next thing you'll want to figure out is your stance width—how far the distance should be from the center of one foot to the center of the other foot. (See illustration page 14.) When it comes to picking a stance width that's right for you, nothing is etched in stone. But if you're new to the sport, it helps to know what other snowboarders are doing. Short kids can ride with stance widths down around 14 inches, while lanky adults might use a width of 24 inches or more. The differences take into account leg length, personal preference, and riding style. Note, however, that use of too wide a stance may cause trouble learning some of the techniques taught in this book.

Most snowboarders plant their feet with a stance width of somewhere between 16 and 24

STANCE WIDTH

If it's your first time trying to figure out how wide your stance should be, try these tricks. They'll provide a good starting point, and you can always adjust the width later. (1) Sit on a bench and measure from the top of your knee to the bottom of your bare heel. Subtract about ½ to 1 inch and you'll have your stance width. (2) Measure your shoulders from outside to outside and use that distance as your stance width.

—*Mike Estes, 1991 Japan Open Halfpipe Champion and 1989 All Japan Mogul Champion*

inches. A narrower stance—favored by racers and some aggressive freeriders—centers your body weight, drives the board downhill faster, and helps carve cleaner turns. Beginners and freestylers lean toward wider stances, which feel more stable and reduce the amount of board swinging out past their feet. Take a look at the chart on this page to see some average stance widths among top pros. Keep in mind that stance widths are different for everybody. Pick what feels best to you and go with it.

Stance Angles

Now that you've got your feet comfortably planted, how do you figure out the proper angle to turn them across the board? Once again, snowboarding is a do-what-you-like sport: turn your feet forward or backward until you hit the angle that feels best to you. If that leaves you scratching your head, here's the lowdown on stance angles.

Stance angle is simply the angle of your feet across the snowboard. (See illustration at right.) If your feet face straight across the board, they're said to be at 0 degrees. If they're parallel with the board, they're at 90 degrees. The stance angles you use depend on the type of riding you do, and vice versa.

If you're going to spend all your time carving turns, it helps to turn your feet forward. This faces your body in the direction you're traveling and opens up your peripheral vision. Racers take this to the extreme by turning their feet forward as much as 60 degrees. When combined with a narrow stance width, this helps racers attain the perfect position for carving turns at high speeds.

Freeriders tone this down a bit, often turning their front foot forward somewhere between 20 and 30 degrees and their back foot forward between 5 and 15 degrees. (Note that the front and back feet have different angles. Most snowboarders turn the front foot farther forward and the back foot more across the board.)

Some freestylers and slopestylers like to have very little stance angle, but this inhibits their ability to make nice turns outside of halfpipes and terrain parks. In general, if you have a zero or negative stance angle on your back foot, you will have a harder time learning how to weight and unweight your turns (more on this later). If it's your first time on a snowboard, take a look at the following chart of average snowboard stances, which provides some average angles used by boarders. Or ask your

AVERAGE SNOWBOARD STANCES

Riding Style or Snowboard	Stance Width (inches)	Stance Angles (degrees)
Freeriding	15 to 20	front: 20 to 30 back: 5 to 15
Halfpipe	18 to 23	front: 10 to 20 back: 0 to 5
Slopestyle	15 to 20	front: 10 to 15 back: 0 to 10
Racing	14 to 18	front: 30 to 55 back: 25 to 55

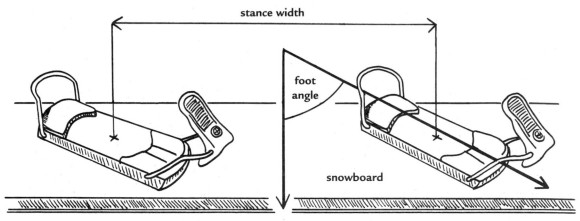

stance width

foot angle

snowboard

*Most snowboards let you change your stance width and stance angles. **Stance width** is the distance between the centers of both feet. **Stance angle** is the angle your bindings are mounted on the snowboard—the larger the angle, the more*

your feet face the front of the snowboard. Experiment with different stance widths and stance angles until you find a combination that's comfortable for you.

shop technician to pick a happy medium for you. Again, you can go more across the board (flatter) if you're riding freestyle, or more up the board (steeper) if you're racing.

Toeside and Heelside Positioning

When setting up your bindings, you generally want to center your feet between the toe and heel edges while keeping your toes and heels from dragging in

the snow. If you have a lot of toe or heel drag, try turning your feet forward a few degrees or using a wider board. You may also want to look for bindings with toe ramps, which will angle your toes higher off the snow. If you have soft boots, you can bevel the soles under the toe and heel to keep them up off the snow—but do it carefully! You wouldn't want to ruin a pair of expensive boots.

Offset

Few beginners should ever fiddle with the placement of their bindings toward the board's tip or tail, other than to adjust their stance width. Manufacturers build boards with certain binding positions in mind, and if you change them, you'll dramatically alter the feel of your board. The only exception to this is something called offset.

Offset is a measure of how far the center of your desired stance is from the center point of the board's length. Almost all snowboarders adjust their bindings in order to shift the center of their stance toward the tail about an inch—for a 1-inch offset—to keep their boards floating. Moving your stance forward, on the other hand—for an offset toward the tip—can help you initiate turns faster. If you have a twin-tip snowboard, the usual stance would be centered, with no offset.

TOE AND HEEL DRAG

Toe and heel drag is just what it says: it's a drag. You can try to eliminate it by angling your bindings slightly forward and adjusting your bindings slightly to the rear, behind the center point of the snowboard. However, if you have really big feet—men's size 12 and above—look for an extra-wide snowboard. These *wide-boards,* pioneered by K2's Fat Bob board, are available from many manufacturers. The wide-board gives riders with big feet a chance to rail on edge just like the alpine race crowd!

—*Charles Arnell*

Looking Good: Snowboarding Apparel

Now that we've discussed everything you need from your ankles down, let's take a U-turn and figure out what you need from your ankles up.

When you first start snowboarding, you'll spend some time on your butt, knees, and hands. Outside your clothes will be an endless supply of cold snow and air anxiously awaiting a chance to chill your skin, while inside your clothes will be a hot body working up a sweat. The same snowy elements that make snowboarding fun can make for a cold, damp, and miserable day if you underdress. So let's take a second to talk about snowboarding apparel.

When picking out jackets and pants, look for clothing that is waterproof and wind resistant. Get outerwear that's roomy enough to allow total free-dom of movement, but watch out for big gaps between tops and bottoms. Also, keep in mind that you may sit or kneel when adjusting your bindings. Therefore, snowboarding pants with waterproof and reinforced seats and knees will last a lot longer than your typical ski pants.

As with any other winter activity, layer your clothes. Start with a thin, close-fitting layer of polypropylene to wick moisture away from your body. Cover your feet with formfitting synthetic socks, and the rest of your body with warm, insulating layers of polypro or wool. Finally, pick a windproof and waterproof outer shell that fits over all of this stuff. Whatever you do, avoid cotton, whether in jeans, T-shirts, or long underwear; cotton loses its insulating properties when it gets cold and wet.

Your hands and fingers will probably take more abuse than any other parts of your body.

Loose, warm, waterproof clothing will keep you comfortable all day long. PHOTO OF J. J. COLLIER BY STEVE WANKE

Thought about wearing a helmet lately? PHOTO (TOP) OF BRIAN DELANEY COURTESY LEEDOM HELMETS; PHOTO (BOTTOM) OF DAN RAY BY RICHARD CHESKI

Remember your head. On cold days, wear a hat to avoid heat loss. On any day, wear ski goggles, sport shields, or sport sunglasses to protect your eyes from UV light, eye-watering winds, and flying snow. If you have to wear prescription lenses when playing in the outdoors, use them on the slopes. You'll see better and you'll ride better. No matter what type of eye protection you choose, carry some antifog spray or no-fog cloths and some eyeglass retainers so that you can see run after run.

Finally, keep a small tube of sunscreen in your pocket when you're snowboarding. High-elevation ski resorts tend to attract sun rays just like a tropical beach, and it's easy to get sunburned without knowing it's happening. Pick a waterproof sunscreen with an SPF of 15 or higher and smear it on regularly. Your skin will thank you for it.

Helmets

When it comes to helmets, you need to make a choice that you are comfortable with, both physically and intellectually. Traditionally, helmets have been used only by the alpine racers who practically fly down the hill at breakneck speeds on closed race courses. You, on the other hand, may someday find yourself on much more dangerous terrain: steep slopes, short cliff faces, and heavily forested runs.

They'll be adjusting bindings every time you get on and off the chairlift, pushing you back up when you lose your balance, and even providing a platform when you're doing handplants in the halfpipe. Choose big, thick, waterproof gloves that'll stand up to the rigors of wet snow and rugged conditions. Fancy leather ski gloves typically won't cut it! Look for snowboarding-specific gloves with durable reinforced fingers and waterproof inserts.

Tailor your clothing and accessories to the weather and type of riding you're doing. Wear thick layers of fleece pants and shirts under your shells to ward off the cold, but dress lightly for warm days. Open up the vents in your clothes if you find yourself sweating hard on the slopes, then zip them back up so you don't get chilled riding the chairlift. Shoot for versatility, and pick styles that make you feel good. If you match your clothing carefully, you'll stay comfortable in all sorts of weather.

Wherever you go, you'll see that helmets are becoming more common on the hills. The hazards of snowboarding certainly justify wearing a helmet, but helmets also limit your peripheral vision and can increase the area of your blind spot.

Whatever your thoughts on helmets are, just know that they are available and that technology is constantly improving them. Each time you snowboard, decide whether you need a helmet—based on your assessment of the conditions, the crowds, and your intentions. And ride safely.

2 On Board
Snowboarding 101

Karine Ruby (France), the gold medalist in the Women's Snowboarding Giant Slalom at the Nagano Winter Olympics in 1998. CHAUN BETTERILL/ALLSPORT

Snowboarding 101. This is where you get to use all that equipment we just talked about. In this chapter we'll practice walking and gliding, turning and stopping—even standing and falling.

If you've got the first-time jitters, relax. You're not alone. Chances are you've spent the better part of your life with your feet planted on solid ground, so you're bound to feel funny standing on a high-tech banana peel.

Novice snowboarders share a broad range of emotions, from unbridled excitement to knee-wobbling fear. Part of the cause is information overload. This chapter is snowboarding's version of learning to drive a car with a clutch—with so many things going on at first, you'll want to scream! But after two or three days on the slopes, you'll turn all that fear and excitement into confidence and

POWER BREAKFAST

The first few days of snowboarding may be more physically demanding than you expect, especially if you're not accustomed to using your newly discovered snowboarding leg and back muscles. Eat an energizing power breakfast before you head out onto the snow. As part of a balanced breakfast, choose foods that are easily digestible and provide readily accessible energy—without making you feel weighted down. Include assorted fruits (melons, bananas, apples) and fruit juices. The energy from this type of breakfast will help keep your body warm and will pump up your leg muscles.

—Charles Arnell

determination. In the end, you'll be ready to move on to chapter 3 and up onto steeper slopes.

Get Ready: Pre-Trip Considerations

If you're fortunate enough to be able to pick the day you start snowboarding, go right after a few inches to a foot of new snow has fallen. A carpet of fresh, spongy, soft-packed snow makes boarding easier—and it provides a giant, natural cushion to catch you if you fall. If possible, don't try to learn snowboarding when conditions are icy. Ice not only makes boarding difficult, it makes falling very painful. But if you have no say in the matter, don some thick clothes and extra padding and go for it!

Gearing Up

I've said it before, and I'll say it again: Today you may fall. Falling is part of the learning process, and something every new snowboarder goes through. Fortunately you're wearing enough warm and waterproof clothing to keep you comfortable and dry.

Whether you're in your van or inside the lodge, start gearing up before you step outside. Wear enough clothing to keep you warm on the chairlift yet comfortable on the slopes. Mix and match layers to accommodate the conditions on the slopes. Once all your clothes are on, pull on your boots. All your foot movements have to make it through the boots to move your board, so make sure the boots are good and snug without cutting off circulation.

The goal is to immobilize your heels so they don't lift or slide around when you're making turns.

Finally, check your equipment to make sure everything is working properly. Are the bindings firmly bolted to the board? Does the leash close securely? Is the stomp pad in place? Are the binding straps and bails in good repair? If you notice a problem with your equipment, take care of it now while you're warm and happy. It will be a pain to fix later.

Warming Up and Stretching

As in any sport, you'll perform better if you warm up and stretch your muscles first. Stretching improves

WARMING UP AND STRETCHING

Start every snowboarding day with warm-up movements to loosen your body and warm the major muscles. Then spend at least ten minutes stretching before you head to the lift line. Stretch out your stomach, back, and neck muscles along with the major leg, arm, and shoulder muscles. If you take the time to stretch, you will feel more relaxed while riding and will be less likely to injure yourself. Another benefit: you won't be as sore and tired at the end of the day.

—Charles Arnell

circulation and stimulates the nerves. Warming up by walking, climbing, or skating for a few minutes has many positive effects. It lubricates your joints and oxygenates your system, it raises the temperature in your muscles and psyches you up, and it also reduces your chances of getting injured.

There is an endless variety of stretching movements from which to choose. Think of the muscle groups you'll be using, and focus on those. Slowly stretch your quadriceps, hamstrings, buttocks, neck, and back. Thoroughly stretch all of the major leg and torso muscles until you feel comfortable and loose. Then stand up and walk around for a few minutes to get your blood pumping again. Once you feel energized, you'll be ready to go.

Beginner Terrain

Snowboarding embraces two very distinct activities working in harmony: reading the mountain and controlling your board. Snowboarding introduces you to wild, three-dimensional landscapes, from neatly groomed hillsides to steep mogul fields. For now, let's tone down the vertical dimension and find a safe, easy haven on which to learn.

For your first run, look for a gentle slope (10 to 15 degrees) with well-groomed, soft-packed snow far from the paths of speeding skiers and snowboarders. The ideal slope will tilt evenly toward a wide, obstacle-free runout and will provide plenty of room to stop. Many ski areas have specially designated bunny slopes with these characteristics. Many bunny slopes add a simple tow—like a rope tow, T-bar, or poma lift—to save your energy for the downhill run, enabling you to learn faster and ride longer.

Snowboarder Anatomy

In chapter 1, we talked about the anatomy of snowboards. Now it's time to discuss the anatomy of snowboarders. Take a look at the photo on page 20. Since snowboarders stand sideways on their boards, each part is described as *front (leading)* or *back (trailing)*. The parts closest to the tip are in front; the parts nearest the tail are in back. Your *front binding* holds your front foot, and your *back binding* holds your back foot. If you're trying to

CARRYING YOUR SNOWBOARD

There are two good ways to carry your board. First, you can carry it under one arm with the bindings facing your body, on either side of your hips. If you carry it this way, you can clip the leash to the back binding to create an over-the-shoulder carrying strap. However, you're better off wrapping the leash around your wrist so the board can't get away.

The second way to carry your board is to rest it against the small of your back, with the bindings facing either in or out. You can hold it there with both arms draped over the base or the deck.

No matter how you carry your board, watch out for other people and objects when you're walking—and don't drop the board. Once it starts sliding, it becomes an uncontrollable missile.

—*Scott Downey*

Here's one way to carry your snowboard. Keep the leash wrapped around your wrist so the board can't get away. COURTESY HIGH CASCADE SNOWBOARD CAMP

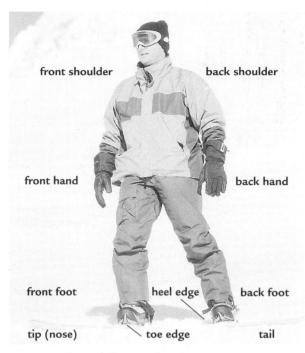

front shoulder   back shoulder

front hand   back hand

front foot   heel edge   back foot

tip (nose)   toe edge   tail

Anatomy of a goofy-foot snowboarder.

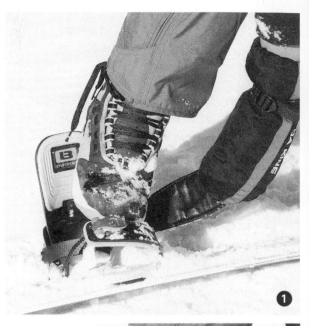

❶

❷

After stepping into a highback binding, tighten the ankle and toe straps just enough to keep your foot firmly in place, but not so tight that they cut off circulation.

find your toe edge or heel edge, just look at your feet. The *toe edge* is under your toes; the *heel edge* is under your heels.

Study the photo before you start boarding. That way, instructions like, "Push your back foot downhill" or "Dig your toe edge into the snow" will make sense.

Buckle Up

The first step in learning to snowboard is learning how to use the bindings. Try this on a broad, flat place. Plop your board down on the snow and take a look at the bindings. How you get into the bindings depends on what type they are.

Highback Bindings (Strap Bindings)

If you have highback bindings and soft boots, here's the best way to buckle in. Let's start with the front binding.

1. Attach the leash to your front leg.
2. Dust the snow out of the front binding.

3. Step into the front binding.
4. Fasten the ankle strap across the top of your foot.
5. Fasten the toe strap (and shin strap, if your binding has one).

If the leash is too short to attach first, secure your front foot before attaching the leash. Tighten the binding just enough to keep your foot firmly in place, but not so tight that it cuts off circulation. If you do this correctly, there'll be no lift between the sole of your boot and the board, and your foot will feel securely nestled in the boot.

Repeat the process for the back binding.

Plate Bindings

If you have hard boots and plate bindings, you'll also start by attaching the leash to your front leg and clearing snow from the bindings. Then you'll follow a slightly different routine. Check whether your binding locks with a heel lever or a toe lever. Here's how to use a plate binding with a toe lever:

1. Insert the heel of your front foot under the front binding's heel bail.
2. Step down with your toe while flipping the toe lever to the locked position.

If the binding has a heel lever, just step in toe first and lock your heel down last.

Repeat the process for the back binding.

Follow the manufacturer's instructions to lock your boot into (or onto) step-in bindings.

Step-in Bindings

Step-ins are designed to be easy to get into and out of. Several types are available. Some of these bindings work by attaching first to one side of the boot, then to the other. Others require that the toe be attached first, then the heel. And still others require that you simply step straight down. Each design has a particular entry movement that is needed in order to engage the boot with the binding.

Some step-in bindings are easier to enter than others. Try them at home or at the rental shop—and practice the engagement movement before you leave for the mountain. Ask the person who set you up with the board to show you how to use the binding if you're at all uncertain about it. Once you figure out how to engage the binding, the process is much easier than strapping in every time you get off the chairlift.

No matter what type of binding you use, remember that whenever you're adjusting

This plate binding uses a toe lever to lock hard boots into place.

them on the slopes, you're a target—a sitting duck—for speeding snowboarders and skiers. Move to the side of the trail to adjust the bindings, and pick a spot where you can be seen by oncoming traffic. If you can avoid it, don't work on the bindings behind a hill or in the middle of a run!

Get Set: Meet Your Snowboard

One of the amazing things about snowboarding is that you can begin training without moving a distance of more than a few feet. Many of the things you'll be doing later—like walking, steering, and balancing on an edge—can be learned on flat ground with only your front foot buckled into the binding. Go ahead and get into the front binding only, and I'll show you what I mean.

Getting Used to Your Board

Once your front foot is buckled in, stand up with your back foot (your free foot) on the snow. Now you're ready to introduce your body to some new sensations—the feelings that come from having a snowboard attached to your front leg.

Pick up your front foot (the one buckled into the binding) and swing the board back and forth to get a feel for its swing weight. Twist it from side to side to see how much it rotates. Try holding it up in front of you and behind you, and see if you can keep it level off the ground. You can even try lifting your loose foot while standing on your front foot.

Are you feeling a little awkward right now? That's normal. Unless you're extraordinarily pigeon-toed, these basic exercises should feel strange. Since you're not used to having one foot pointing inward so much, your body will automatically try to straighten out that front foot. Your goal is to keep the board straight and to resist the urge to straighten your front foot. This will be easier if you keep your knees slightly bent. In time, your pigeon-toed walking stance will become second nature and you'll feel comfortable using it whenever you're walking, skating, or resting on a chairlift.

Sliding

The next step is to practice sliding your snowboard across the snow. Start off with a relaxed, upright stance. Keep your head up, and look forward to keep your balance. Try to keep most of your body weight on the foot that is attached to the snowboard.

Walking with your front foot buckled in will feel strange at first. Soon, it will become second nature.

Keep your back foot in the middle of the stomp pad when gliding with just your front foot buckled in.

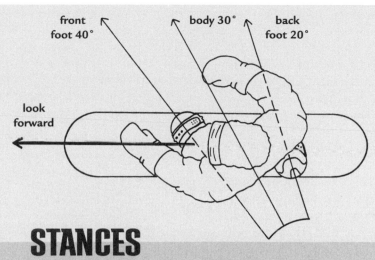

front foot 40°   body 30°   back foot 20°

look forward

*A comfortable, efficient **stance** is very important when you're learning to snowboard. You shouldn't feel tight, rigid, or twisted. To find a comfortable stance, first look forward while keeping your chest at right angles to your feet. From that position you can easily turn more forward or sideways to suit your riding style.*

STANCES

A balanced athletic stance is a must for proper snowboarding technique. Position your feet with angles that allow your body to aggressively move fore and aft along the length of the snowboard. Choose foot angles that allow your upper torso to be perpendicular to the centerline of the snowboard. Your trailing hand should be driving forward just like your leading hand. This position will allow you to make equal and similar body movements for both your toeside and heelside turns.

—*Charles Arnell*

With your loose foot still stationary on the snow, push the board back and forth and side to side. As you become more comfortable and balanced, bend your knees and flex your ankles. You'll soon find that the board skids easily when you're standing tall, but that the edges *catch* or *slice* the snow when you tilt the board up on one edge. In a little while, you'll use this slicing action to keep the board under control as you learn to walk with it. Ultimately the edges will help you turn when you're riding down the slopes.

Balancing

By now you're probably pretty good at moving the board around while standing on your free foot, so let's make things more challenging. As your confidence grows, keep moving closer to getting both feet on the board. When you're ready, put your back foot on the stomp pad and assume a relaxed stance, facing forward with your head up. Your arms should feel relaxed, with hands just above the hips.

Once you find your comfortable stance, you can try a couple of exercises to improve your balance. First, crouch down and stand up using just your knees (try not to bend at the waist). Next, try standing on your front foot, with your back foot off the ground behind you. Keep all of your weight over your front foot and use your arms for balance. Gradually you'll find your equilibrium. And muscles you didn't even know existed will let you know they're working.

Edging

With both feet still on the board, rock it from edge to edge. Keep your head up and look out toward the horizon. Just feel the board, without staring down at it.

Starting with your toe edge, stand upright and relaxed as you lift your heels and roll onto the balls of both feet. The heel edge should lift off the snow while the toe edge digs in. Pay attention to the rest of your body: your hips will cross the center of the board to maintain your balance, and you may feel some boot pressure against the tops of your ankles or shins. That's good—you're doing things right.

Once you get the feel for your toe edge, rock back onto your heels and dig the heel edge into the snow. Again, pay attention to your body: your hips will rock backward slightly, and you may feel some boot pressure on top of your toes or behind your calves.

Experiment to find your balance point by flexing your knees, hips, and ankles, and don't worry if you fall down. When you start riding, you'll always be on one edge or the other, so practice until you're comfortable. Soon you'll be able to turn the board slightly onto either edge without falling over.

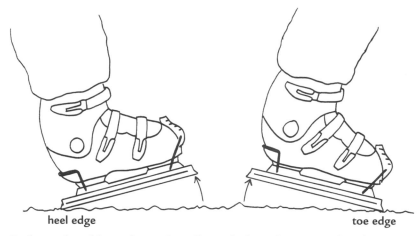

heel edge   **toe edge**

Rock your board from edge to edge. Lift your heels to tilt your snowboard up onto the toe edge, and lift your toes to roll your snowboard onto the heel edge. As you practice balancing on one edge at a time, pay attention to the pressures your boots exert on your feet, ankles, and calves. Later on, you'll spend most of your time riding on one edge or the other.

Center of Mass

Now it's time to learn about your center of mass—an imaginary point somewhere between your belly

*Your **center of mass** is an imaginary point (see circles above) somewhere between your belly button and tailbone. Move your center of mass backward (left photo) and forward (right photo) by sliding your hips toward the tip or the tail of snowboard. Resist the urge to bend at your waist.*

lower back. If you're really good, you can balance over the board's tip or tail without falling over.

When you're done with these exercises, you should have an appetite for greater challenges. If you're still shaky, back off a bit and work on what you've learned. You'll get the hang of it!

Go: Do the Snowboard Shuffle

Walking with just your front foot buckled to the board is an essential skill—as much a part of snowboarding as carving turns. You'll walk in lift lines, when you get off lifts, and anytime you want to get somewhere without unbuckling your bindings.

Take your first step with your weight centered over the front foot and your feet close together. Next, pretend you're on a skateboard or a scooter: keep your weight on the leg at-

1

Walking with a snowboard is similar to pushing a skateboard or a scooter. Start with your weight on your front foot, with your feet close together (1). To slide the board forward, push your free foot backward (2). Take tiny steps at first and keep the board tilted on its toe edge to keep it from sliding out. As you improve, you can take bigger steps (3).

2

button and your tailbone. Snowboarders pay a lot of attention to their center of mass because it helps determine which end of the snowboard travels downhill first. For example, sliding your center of mass forward and flattening the board helps the board turn downhill from a traverse. (If you were to slide your center of mass toward the tail in the same situation, you might head down the hill backward.)

Move your center of mass around by sliding your hips and torso toward the tip of the board, then toward the tail. Don't *lean* forward; instead, *slide* your hips forward and keep your upper body over them.

Go a little farther each time and see how it feels. The movement of your upper body should come from your legs rocking and not from your

3

tached to the snowboard as you push gently with the free foot.

Take tiny, controlled steps and try to slide the board without picking it up off the snow. As you become more agile, increase the size of your steps. Try walking with your loose foot on either side of the board. And try walking in circles and walking in figure eights. Later on, these exercises will help you maneuver your board in tight spots—like crowded lift lines.

Walking Uphill

Since this is the first time you've actually been on a hill with your snowboard—even though you're going uphill—you need to know about the fall line. This is an imaginary line that traces the steepest slope down any given hill. If that explanation doesn't make sense, try this one: Pretend you're standing on top of a hill with a ball. Let the ball go and see where it rolls. Whether it follows a straight path or winds its way downhill, the ball will always roll down the fall line. We'll talk about fall lines a lot from here on out, so think about the concept for a minute and check out the accompanying diagram.

To begin your walk uphill, place the snowboard across the fall line and plant your loose foot uphill. Bend your knees to dig the toe edge into the snow, and step forward with your loose foot. Each time you step forward, lift and drag the board

To walk uphill, tilt the snowboard on its toe edge and step forward with your loose foot. Drag the snowboard uphill behind you with each step.

uphill behind you (as if you're walking with a ball and chain), then replant the toe edge in the snow. It isn't pretty, but it sure is functional.

Skating

With all this practice, you're probably comfortable enough to try skating. Skating isn't much different from walking; it just adds short glides in place of a few extra steps. Skating does, however, demand a little more balance and attention to the terrain. Pick a place with a smooth, shallow slope to learn how to skate.

Skating starts the same way as your first walking step: place most of your weight over the front foot and push with the back foot. As your board starts to slide, put the back foot on the middle of the stomp pad and briefly glide with both feet on the board. If you have trouble keeping the board gliding straight, try pointing your lead arm over the nose of the board. This action will help you to properly weight the front foot and keep the board gliding straight.

It'll take some time before you're good at skating, so build up gradually. Once it becomes easy, try pushing with your back foot on either side of the board, alternating sides each time the foot hits the ground.

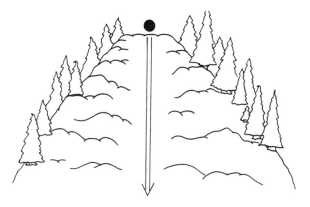

*The **fall line** is an imaginary line that traces the steepest part of any given slope. It is the same path a ball would take if you rolled it down a hill.*

HOPPING

Sooner or later you're going to find a place—such as a deep patch of fresh powder—where both feet are buckled in, and walking won't work. When that happens, you can hop from one spot to another with this technique:

Place your palms on the snow in front of you and pull your knees and feet up under your chest. Next, spring up and forward like a frog. You can drag your hands on the snow, or hop up high with each jump.

Hopping also works great on flatter, harder snow: all you have to do is hop standing up by jumping forward with both feet at the same time.

—*Scott Downey*

You can hop like a frog to move uphill quickly or to get out of deep powder.

Steering and Pivoting

We're now going to do some pivoting and walking exercises to learn basic motions that will go into your first turns. With both feet on the snowboard, use your hips and legs to spin your feet to the left, then to the right. The ends of the board will swing back and forth and cut a big X into the snow. This is pivoting.

When you're comfortable pivoting, gradually move the center of the X (the *pivot point*) from the middle of your feet to your front foot by putting a little more weight on the front foot and use your back foot to execute the pivoting motion. When you make your first skidded turns, this same motion will be used to help forcefully steer your board through rudimentary turns. As you become more experienced and learn to carve your turns in a more refined manner, you'll still find occasions when steering can help you execute quick turns in a pinch.

Walking in large circles or figure eights—pushing with your free foot—can also teach some basic steering motions involved in turning. First, walk in the direction your front toes are pointing, keeping your free foot in front of your toe edge. Once you're comfortable with that routine, walk in the

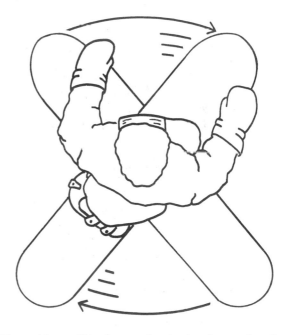

Try making an X in the snow by pivoting the snowboard back and forth in one place. This will start to teach your legs how to move the snowboard, improve your feel for the board's edges, and get you ready for the slopes. Pivoting will gradually disappear as you learn to move your body as one unit through a turn, then will reappear when you learn hockey-style stops.

direction that your front heel is pointing, keeping your free foot behind your heel edge.

These exercises teach you to guide the tip in the direction you want to go and force you to use the edge closest to the inside of the turn. Practice them until they seem second nature, and turning will be easier to learn.

The Joy of Gravity: Riding Downhill

Snowboarding is a gravity sport. The same force that pulled the apple down on Newton's head pulls snowboarders down the slopes. Skilled snowboarders thrive on gravity. With it, they rip down groomed trails at blazing speeds and blast off jumps that leave them dizzy with adrenaline.

A popular myth is that snowboarding is the same as skateboarding or surfing. There is some truth to this, but snowboard turning movements actually have more in common with snow skiing than with skateboarding or surfing. Skateboards and surfboards are propelled by forces pushing from behind, while snowboarding is a gravity sport. This means that the methods of controlling movement and of steering are very different.

In skateboarding and surfing, you steer by initiating turns with the rear foot. In snowboarding you initiate the turning motion with the front leg.

If you try to ride the snowboard like a surfboard or skateboard—putting your weight on the rear foot and trying to initiate the turn from the rear—you'll find your board turning sideways, turning backward, and catching edges with little warning. Though snowboarding has roots in surfing, skateboarding, and snow skiing, it helps to understand both the similarities and differences among these sports.

At this point, you've got the basics pretty well under control. You've already learned about equipment, safety, how to use your bindings, and how to walk and to skate. If you're feeling pretty good, you're probably ready for your first downhill glide. If your knees are still shaking like willows in a gale, relax. Proceed at your own pace. Go back to some flat terrain and work on basic skills until you feel genuinely comfortable, then come on along. It's time to put both feet on the board and let gravity do the work.

Straight Glide

Find a short, shallow slope with plenty of runout for your first glide. With only your front foot buckled in, point the board downhill, let gravity help you begin gliding, and gradually work your loose foot onto the stomp pad. Look forward, keep a relaxed stance, and put a little more weight on your *front foot*. If you start to slide or turn backward, it's probably because too much weight is on your back foot.

Expect the unexpected on your first glide. You might make it to the bottom of the slope, or you might fall. If you do fall, keep your back foot *on the board*! This is a good habit to develop now, since you can easily injure your legs by stepping on the ground when your board is moving.

On my first couple of glides, I kept spinning backward. The same thing might happen to you. Riding backward is something that sets snowboarding apart from skiing and makes it more versatile. If you do it now, it's called a surprise. Later on—when you get good—riding backward is called riding *fakie* or *switch stance*. For now, just keep a little more weight over your front foot and you should keep gliding forward.

Once you're accustomed to gliding with just your front foot in the binding, buckle both feet in and try it again. You'll have to throw your center of mass forward to get going. Remember, your center of mass is down low, near your stomach. It's not in your head—at least for most people—or between your shoulders. So don't just lean forward at your waist. Throw your hips forward. If you can't get your board to move, pick a better starting place.

Once you get going, keep your weight forward and use your back foot to steer. (That's what the steering practice was all about!) Keep looking where you want to go, and enjoy the ride.

You might not realize it until the bottom of the run—but you're now snowboarding!

THE HANDY PLATFORM

If you're unable to find a flat spot to buckle into your bindings or to stand up, sit facing downhill and bulldoze out a small platform by pushing the snow up with your board. The platform makes a great place to finish buckling up the bindings, and gives you a place to stand before starting your run.

—*Scott Downey*

Falling

Folks who have never snowboarded sometimes shudder at stories of broken wrists, hands, and ankles. Fortunately these injuries are rare and they're often preventable if you know how to fall.

The first thing to do when falling is to make fists so you don't jam your hands or wrists into the snow. If you fall toeside, let your forearms touch first, then land on your stomach. If you fall toward your heelside, let your butt touch down first and slide to a stop on your back. Whichever way you fall, keep your board up off the snow so it doesn't catch and cause sudden, painful stops.

Don't be embarrassed to wear knee pads, wrist guards, or butt pads if falling worries you. They'll make your first few days of snowboarding safer and more comfortable and they

may improve your learning curve by boosting your confidence.

Standing Up

You can stand up from either a kneeling or a sitting position. If you're *kneeling*, face uphill with the board behind you. Be sure the board is straight across the fall line, or you'll slide sideways every time you try to stand. Pull your heels up under your butt and dig your toe edge into the snow. At the same time, work your hands back toward the outside of your knees. Before you stand up, look uphill and check for oncoming traffic. When the coast is clear, push up with your arms and straighten your legs. You're standing!

TOESIDE AND HEELSIDE TURNS

Stance	Toeside Turn	Heelside Turn
Regular	Right Turn	Left Turn
Goofy	Left Turn	Right Turn

Standing up on your board's heel edge can be a little harder than standing up on the toe edge. To rise to a standing position on the heel edge, pull the snowboard close to your body and dig the heel edge in the snow. Reach across and grab the toe edge with your back hand. To stand up, rock forward over the board, pull with your arm, and straighten your legs.

When sitting in deep powder or on a flat slope (1), it is sometimes easier to roll over onto your board's toe edge (2 and 3) before standing up.

If you're *sitting down*, facing downhill, you can roll over onto your knees and stand up on your toes, or you can stand up on your heel edge. To stand on your heel edge, pull your feet up close to your body and dig your heel edge into the snow (see photo page 29). When you're ready to stand, reach across and grab the front toe edge with your back hand. To stand up, rock forward, pull with your arm, and straighten your legs.

Don't worry if you plop back down a couple of times before you remain upright. Standing up is just like any other skill—it takes a little practice.

Toeside and Heelside Turns

Regular and *goofy* stances can make snowboard lessons confusing. What seems normal to a goofy rider seems backward to a regular rider, and vice versa. So let's take a minute to discuss what different stances do to our turning lessons.

Snowboarders talk about only two ways to turn: *toeside* and *heelside*. (The turns are also referred to as frontside and backside.) Both turns are just what they say: toeside turns take you onto your toe-side edge, and heelside turns take you onto your heelside edge.

If that doesn't make sense, here's everything you'll ever need to know on the subject: If you're regular, toeside turns are right turns, and heelside turns are left turns. If you're goofy, toeside turns are left turns, and heelside turns are right turns.

YOUR FIRST SKIDDED TURN

Stay on a short, gentle slope with a flat runout to practice your first skidded turn. That will give you a chance to learn a basic turn *before* you have to ride the chairlift. If you're going to ride the chairlift *first*, skip ahead to chapter 4 and read the sections on sideslipping and traversing techniques. Those techniques will help you feel more comfortable when you're staring down upon your first beginner slope.

—Scott Downey

③

④

Skidded Turns

There are three types of snowboard turns: *skidded turns* (in which your feet actively steer the board), *carved turns* (using the board's sidecut and flex to turn), and *jump turns* (turning the board while airborne). Before the days of metal edges and sidecut, skidded turns and jump turns were the only way to control snowboards. However, today's snowboards are built to carve like skis.

Skidded turns are the first step toward learning carved turns. Skidded turns teach balance and edge control at slower speeds by using more base than edge. Once you master skidded turns, you'll be ready to turn the board high on its edge and carve with abandon.

Three actions work in harmony to make the snowboard turn: you *look* in the direction you want to turn, *weight* the front foot, and *tilt* the board on its turning edge. As the board *(continued page 34)*

SKIDDED TURNS

Both feet are important in making smooth skidded turns. If you think of your front foot as your *gas* and your back foot as your *brake*, skidded turns will be a little easier to execute.

Whenever you want to glide down the fall line, slide more weight forward over your front foot as you flatten the board onto the snow.

When you're ready to turn, steer the board by pressing your back foot downhill. Don't kick your back foot downhill to pivot your snowboard unless you have to. The cleanest skidded turns arc gently through the snow with both feet controlling the snowboard

—John Calkins, Professional Ski Instructors of America (PSIA) member and Technical Director of High Cascade Snowboard Camp

*Three actions work together to start any **skidded turn:** you look in the direction you want to turn, weight your front foot, and tilt the board onto its turning edge. As you start turning, you can steer with your feet and balance on your uphill edge to cross the slope.*

goofy, heelside turn

goofy, toeside turn

A regular-foot boarder makes a toeside skidded turn.

(continued from page 34) rolls onto the uphill edge, you steer through the turn by using your feet to control the steering. Let's put all three actions—looking, weighting, and tilting—together and see what happens.

Make your first skidded turn with your front foot buckled in and your back foot on the stomp pad. (This is exactly how you'll get off chairlifts.) Start at the top of a shallow slope with a relaxed stance and your hands about waist high. Begin a straight downhill glide and slide more of your weight forward onto your front foot. (Remember: move your hips forward, don't just lean.) Once you have a little speed, you're ready to make your first turn.

Toeside turns are the easiest to learn (they use the more powerful calf muscles, ankles, and toes), so let's do them first. To begin a toeside turn, *look* where you want to turn, slide more *weight* onto your front foot, and *tilt* your weight onto the balls of both feet. That should be enough to get the board turning. As it begins to turn, sink slightly into the board by bending your knees, and gently push your back leg downhill to steer. The snowboard will leave the fall line and cross the hill. If you stand equally on the balls of both feet, you'll ease into a slow, gentle traverse. To stop, keep turning uphill, but don't turn too far. You may start sliding again—backward!

Heelside turns are executed almost the same way. *Look* over your front shoulder into the turn, slide your *weight* onto the front foot, and *tilt* back onto your heel edge. As the board begins to turn, sink into the board by bending your knees, and steer by gently pushing your back leg downhill. Traverse with your weight spread evenly between both feet, and push the back leg downhill a bit more to stop.

Three tips will help you improve quickly once you figure out how to do skidded turns: First, listen to the sound of your turns. An even, uniform skidding sound means you're turning smoothly. Second, steer from the start (as soon as you begin dropping down the fall line) so that you don't have to brake and pivot all at once. As you improve, you can steer the board evenly throughout the entire turn. Finally, *practice, practice, practice.* Nobody says you have to learn skidded turns in fifteen minutes, an hour, or even your first day. Go at your own pace, but keep at it. Once that first magical turn happens, you'll never look back.

Stopping

The first question most people think of as soon as their feet are attached to a snowboard is, "How do I stop this thing?" Think what it would be like to be in a car, rolling downhill, with no brakes. Make you nervous? It ought to. How about gliding down a steep incline without knowing how to stop? No thanks!

Until now, everything you've learned involves movement: walking, skating, gliding, and turning. However, the ability to stop your board is just as important as any other skill, especially when getting off lifts, entering lift lines, or coming upon obstacles during a run. So let's talk about stopping the board—with and without style.

To come to a stop as you glide down the slope (1), turn the board perpendicular to the fall line (2), tilt the board hard on the uphill edge (3), and balance over both feet.

Any beginner can tell you the easiest way to stop: drop to your butt and skid to a halt. The butt drop varies in effectiveness depending on your starting speed and the snow you're landing on. Sometimes you'll brake slowly, other times you'll break your butt. Most of the time, there's a better way.

Look at the photo sequence on skidded turns on pages 32 and 33. Notice that every boarder is entering a traverse from a straight glide using the same techniques: they pressure their uphill edge, then gently slide their back foot down the hill. That's almost identical to stopping.

To stop, turn the board perpendicular to the fall line, tilt the board hard on the uphill edge, and balance over both feet. (See photos page 35.) You can do this slowly, just as you did in skidded turns, or quickly, by swiveling your hips and kicking your back foot downhill. (Remember our pivoting exercise?) With practice, you'll eventually be able to skid to lightning-fast stops just like hockey players on ice skates.

3 The Big Picture
How to Use Ski Areas

DENNIS CURRAN/SPORTS FILE

You're still here? Great! If you've made it this far, chances are you're about to become a bona fide snowboarder. Before we start handing out diplomas, however, we need to learn a new batch of skills. Skills like traversing, carving turns, and handling changing terrain. These skills are best learned and practiced on steeper, longer slopes, with chairlifts or surface tows to save our energy for the descents.

This chapter is your introduction to ski areas, resort etiquette, and lifts. It also introduces you to the snowboarders and skiers sharing the slopes with you. It whisks you from the bunny slopes, straight into the lift lines, and on up the hill. Along the way, you'll learn how to make sense out of the mountain maze, follow ski area customs, and how to snowboard safely.

The Lay of the Land: Ski Areas

Until now, we've spent all of our time on the bunny slopes safely hidden from the steady stream of experienced snowboarders and skiers carving up the trails. However, you now have the tools to move out onto groomed beginner trails without having to worry. The question is, how do you know where the beginner trails are? The answer takes us to the design of a typical ski area.

Whether you're snowboarding in the Rockies or Sierras, the Cascades or the Appalachians, ski areas are remarkably similar. Almost every resort has one or more lodges, chairlifts, rope tows, groomed trails, and ungroomed trails. It is the ever-changing combination of these features that makes each resort unique, while their similarities fill us with feelings of familiarity and security.

Lodges

Almost every ski area has one or more day lodges. Nestled in the valley close to major trails and chairlifts, day lodges are the hub of mountain activity. This is where snowboarders can find ticket counters, rental centers, snowboard schools, gift shops, and restaurants. Larger resorts may even have lodges halfway up the mountain or at the summit of popular trails.

No matter where the lodges are, make the main lodge your first stop when you get to the resort. You can learn a lot about the ski area by just poking around, reading signs and plaques, and picking up some informative literature.

Bunny Slopes

Once you walk outside the main lodge, it's usually just a short walk back to familiar grounds—the bunny slopes. Bunny slopes are usually located close to the lodge so that first-timers can duck back inside whenever they need a healthy dose of interior comfort. You're also still in the valley, so the gentle slopes near the lodge provide ideal terrain for novice boarders.

Trails

Major trails and chairlifts usually radiate from the main valley and day lodges like spokes in a wagon wheel. Whether the lifts service every run on one mountain, or hook you up with lifts that service other slopes, they are the lifeblood of the ski resort.

The layout of the trail system depends on the mountain's terrain and obstacles. However, some common patterns begin to emerge the more places you snowboard. Beginner runs are usually on the lowest part of the mountain. Chances are, they're also the closest runs to the main lodge. The higher you go on the mountain, the more likely you are to see intermediate, advanced, and expert terrain. Still, that doesn't mean that every ski area is laid out like a layer cake, with the toughest runs on top and the easiest runs on the bottom. To make sure you don't find yourself on a trail that's above your skill level, familiarize yourself with trail signs, and learn how to read a trail map.

Trail Signs: The International Trail Marking System

The International Trail Marking System uses three symbols to explain the degree of difficulty for each trail. The easiest trails are marked with a *green circle*, more difficult trails with a *blue square*, and the most difficult trails with a *black diamond*. (Some ski areas have a handful of expert-only runs, which are marked by *double black diamonds* to keep run-of-the-mill "experts" away.)

Since the symbols only compare the difficulty of runs on that mountain, start off on the easiest trails and work your way up. Nothing's worse than picking an intermediate trail on a steep mountain, only to find out that it's twice as hard as the expert runs on your local hill. Plus, starting easy gives your legs a chance to warm up before you head for steeper runs.

On any given day, a trail can become easier or more difficult than indicated. On deep powder days, a flat trail becomes more difficult and the steep hills easier. On cold, icy days just about every

Trail signs point the way to the trails on the mountain. COURTESY MT. BACHELOR SKI AND SUMMER RESORT

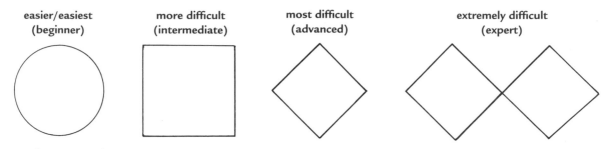

North American ski resorts use green circles, blue squares, and black diamonds to explain the degree of difficulty for most trails.

trail can have some challenging terrain. When extreme weather sets in, the light can go very flat, and whiteout conditions can occur, with very limited visibility. Since dramatic changes in the slope lighting, cloud cover, and weather patterns can make any trail "most difficult" at any time, be aware of the conditions each and every day you go snowboarding.

There are many signs beyond circles, squares, and diamonds, each of which make your snowboarding adventures safer.

Signs with the word "slow" on them are usually posted wherever there's a lot of traffic. This may be near chairlifts, lodges, or wherever popular runs converge. Keep your eyes open when coming into slow zones, and slow down!

Signs warning of "danger" usually show an exclamation point inside a triangle. These signs warn snowboarders that hazards—such as cliffs, large boulders, or fragile cornices—are present. Slow down whenever you see them, and steer clear of the danger.

Signs that display a plus sign are usually posted at first-aid and ski patrol facilities.

When an area of the mountain is closed, it may be marked with a sign that says "closed," or with a graphic of a skier in a red circle with a red diagonal slash across it.

Understand what each sign means before you go snowboarding. If you aren't sure, ask someone. This is especially important if you go snowboarding internationally. Resorts in Europe have signs marked in several different European languages, and in Japan they are marked in the kanji characters of the Japanese language. In these cases, pay extra attention to the color of the marking and any picture or diagram that helps explain the signs.

The Mountain Menu: Trail Maps

Whenever you're on an unfamiliar mountain, grab a trail map before heading out onto the slopes. These maps are your guide to the trails, chairlifts, lodges, and patrol stations. Think of them as mountain menus, and choose the courses that look the most appetizing.

Rules of the Road: The Skier Responsibility Code

When I'm out on the slopes, it's just me, my board, and the snow. The world fades to a blur, and nothing else seems to matter—until some self-proclaimed winter dynamo barrels over my toe edge at 40 miles per hour and sends me cartwheeling into oblivion.

Ski trails are the mountain's human highways. If you're the only one out there, you can pretty much do as you please. But the second you add people, the chances of collisions and injuries increase.

The *skier responsibility code* (along with its snowboard translation) guides our peaceful coexistence with fellow snowboarders and skiers. There are many variations of this code, but these six core provisions are common everywhere:

Pick up a trail map before heading out onto the slopes. Trail maps are your guide to the trails, chairlifts, lodges, and patrol stations. COURTESY MT. BACHELOR SKI AND SUMMER RESORT

1. Ski under control and in such a manner that you can stop or avoid other skiers or objects. (If you see a skier or snowboarder, turn. Trees too.)

2. When skiing downhill or overtaking another skier, you must avoid the skier below you. (Don't run skiers down. Launch airs in places where you can see who may be in your way.)

3. You must not stop where you obstruct a trail or are not visible from above. (If you sit down during a run, do it on the side of the trail. You'll be less likely to get hit.)

4. When entering a trail or starting downhill, yield to other skiers. (Crashing into others could hurt someone. Look uphill when entering a run and check your blind spot when traversing.)

5. All skiers shall use devices to help prevent runaway skis. (Always wear your leash when you're walking, skating, or riding. Wrap it around your wrist or leave it on your leg when carrying your board.)

6. You shall keep off closed trails and posted areas and observe all posted signs. (Don't cut ropes and go out of bounds, even though there may be some awesome powder out there. You may get a big fine, lose your pass, or worse, get snuffed by an avalanche.)

The six-point skier responsibility code is just a starting point for safe snowboarding. Here are some more safety tips to think about:

- Remember that you've got a blind spot behind your back. Pay attention to others around you and be aware of their intentions. The more you know about other snowboarders and skiers, the better you can predict their moves.

- The skier or snowboarder who is downhill always has the right of way. Yield when passing, and yell *left* or *right* to let that person know which side you're going to pass on.

- Before trying any maneuver in the midst of other snowboarders or skiers, check to see where other people are and where you might end up.

- Let snow conditions, crowd size, and safety considerations dictate your snowboarding.

- Respect the safety rules and programs of the mountain staff.

- Slow down before you enter a crowded area so that you can stop quickly if you have to.

- Never jump where you can't see the landing.

- If you are involved in an accident, stop and offer assistance. (If you don't, you might be criminally liable.) If you see an accident, report it to the ski patrol.

- Snowboard with a friend whenever you're in the trees, deep powder, or off the beaten track. Stay in visual and voice contact.

- Watch out for snow cats and stay away from snow guns.

- Be a good ambassador of the sport. Don't antagonize the locals, skiers, or the mountain management.

Lifts

Now that we've covered everything from fundamental skills to safety and etiquette, we're ready to try some longer runs on steeper trails. They're a little higher up the mountain, so we'll have to use a lift to get to them. The lifts cut all of the climbing work out of snowboarding, but can scare the fleece off a beginner. With a few tips and some practice, however, you'll be able to handle all kinds of lifts with ease.

Surface Lifts

First, let's talk about surface lifts: *rope tows, J-bars, T-bars*, and *poma lifts (platter lifts)*. You ride all of these surface lifts with your front foot buckled in and your leash attached. The good part about this is that you're basically gliding straight up the mountain while the lift does all the work. The bad part is that your back leg is loose and could catch the snow. Since the lift zips along pretty fast, catching your back foot can cause an injury. Keep your back foot firmly planted on the stomp pad, and leave it there—even if you fall! Your legs will thank you for it.

Rope Tows

A rope tow is a continuous loop of moving rope. To use a rope tow, skate into position and point your snowboard uphill. Lightly grab the rope and slowly tighten your grip until the rope starts tugging you along. To keep from flopping forward, lean back a bit and keep your knees bent. If you fall, don't sweat it. Let go of the rope, crawl out of the way, and buckle your back foot in. You can ride your snowboard back to the starting area and give it another shot. If you make it to the top, skate away from the unloading zone, and go have fun!

J-Bars

J-bars are hook-shaped bars that rest behind you and pull you up the hill. Even though they look like crude seats, don't try to sit on them—they won't support your weight. Just place the bottom of the bar behind you, lean back a bit, and prepare for a bit of a jolt. Once you get moving, ride your board as if you were making a straight glide.

T-Bars

T-bars are very similar to J-bars, but are designed to pull two people uphill at a time. Like J-bars, T-bars hang from an overhead cable on spring-loaded lines that reel out under the pressure of your body weight. If you make the mistake of sitting down on the T-bar at the starting line, the spring-loaded line will start the T-bar up the hill, but you'll fall over backward. All of this makes T-bars a little trickier than your average rope tow or J-bar, so stand back and check them out before you actually try them.

Poma Lifts

Poma lifts were built for skiers—not snowboarders—but they work just fine for us anyway. Rather than sticking the platter between your legs like a skier would, just grab hold of it with your hands and use it like a rope tow.

Chairlifts

Surface lifts are fine when you're first starting out, but they wear out your arms and suck away energy that could be better spent snowboarding. That's where chairlifts come in. Chairlifts are great. You get to sit down, relax, and check out the scenery from a bird's-eye view while the chairlift carries you to the top of the trail. All you have to do is get on and off the lift in perfect balance.

To the novice snowboarder, chairlifts present a unique

When exiting the chairlift, first place your board on the snow pointing straight, then put your back foot on the stomp pad (1). As you stand on the board, look straight ahead as you glide downward (2, 3). (Come to a stop before walking or skating away to a safer location, away from the lift ramp and crowds, to buckle up.)

Once you've figured out how the T-bar works, give it a try. Skate to the starting line and wait for one of the lift operators to hand you the T-bar. Place it behind your butt and maintain a relaxed, upright stance. Use your hands to grab the line or upright bar. Now, bend your knees and glide up the track to the top of the hill. When you reach the top, watch out! If you're not careful, the T-bar will recoil upward and bonk you in the head. Before you skate away from the unloading area, use your inside hand to guide the T-bar over the safety gate. On your first attempt ask the lift attendant if you may go up alone. This will help you gain confidence and control before you have to ride up with a stranger sporting brand new skis that he doesn't want scratched!

paradox: they save you hours of climbing by effortlessly carrying you up the slopes, but they can unceremoniously dump you on the exit ramp at the end of the ride. During my first days on a snowboard, I skidded, wallowed, and rolled off chairlifts in ways that would have made circus tumblers green with envy. After one particularly humorous fall, a fellow snowboarder came up and said, "Geez, bro', that was pretty sick. All ya gotta do is keep your weight on your front foot, your back foot on the board, and . . ."

I added his advice to everything else people were telling me, buckled in, and made another run. Halfway through my next chairlift ride, his words came back to me: "Keep your weight on your front foot, back foot on the board." I looked at the upcoming exit ramp and prepared for another fall. But this time, I made my first smooth exit of the morning!

The point here is that chairlifts aren't really that big of a deal if you know what to do.

There are many different types of chairlifts. There are two-seaters (*doubles*), three-seaters (*triples*) and four-seaters (*quads*). Some chairlifts are fast, some are slow. Some have foot bars, some don't. Some have shields that swing overhead to block the cold, others are open-air. No matter how many chairs or accessories your chairlift has, the techniques involved are pretty much the same.

To start out, skate up to the loading line quickly and look backward so that you can see the chair coming. When it gets to you, sit all the way back in the seat, keep your board pointed straight, and keep your back foot up in front of you. (Don't let the board or your back foot catch under the chair!) Once on the chair, relax and enjoy the trip. If you watch other snowboarders, mentally critique their techniques or watch them to pick up a few new tricks.

When you near the unloading platform, scoot forward on the chair (don't fall off!) and point your board straight ahead. Lift the tip up so it doesn't catch the unloading platform, and put your back foot over the stomp pad. Now, make sure your board is still straight and that your back foot lands on the stomp pad when the board hits the snow. Put both hands on the edge of the seat and use them to guide you to a standing position.

NO MORE ACHING FEET

Since your board hangs from your front foot when you're riding a chairlift, the front leg and instep can get sore. A handy trick is to let the board rest on top of your back foot. This spreads the weight evenly over both feet and makes for a more comfortable ride.

—*Scott Downey*

Rest your snowboard on top of your back foot when riding a chairlift to save wear and tear on your front leg.

Now you can glide down the unloading ramp under control. If you can, turn away from unloading traffic, or glide to a stop and skate away.

Whatever you do, don't put your back foot down on the snow while getting off the chair. Keep it on the board, even if you fall. Otherwise you might get hurt.

The best chair to learn on is a detachable quad chair or any chair that slows down for the entry and exit of passengers. These detachable chairs usually have shallow exit ramps and are nonthreatening. Unfortunately most ski areas do not have these detachable chairs on the bunny slopes. If this is the case where you learn, keep this thought in mind: if you can survive the chair on the bunny hill, the rest of the chairs should be a piece of cake!

Lift Lines

If you happen to be on a popular mountain on a perfect day, plan on spending some time in lift lines. Some lines can last half an hour or more. If you're lucky, you can get in line, on the lift, and back up the mountain in no time flat.

When approaching the lift line, pull out of the path of traffic, slow to a stop, and undo your back binding. Don't try to ride up the line; skate in with one foot out. Be polite and don't ride over anyone else's equipment. When you get to the front of the line, have your pass visible and be ready to move. If it's your first time riding the lift, let the operators know. They'll usually explain how to load safely and may slow the lift down to make your life easier.

Other Ways of Getting Up the Mountain

Surface lifts and chairlifts aren't the only way to reach the top of the mountain. At some ski areas (especially in Europe), gondolas, trams, and cable cars transport skiers and boarders from valleys to the top of the ski area. These enclosed lifts can carry anywhere from a couple of people to a small crowd. All riders have to remove their skis and snowboards before climbing aboard.

It's important to obey all of the rules for riding these types of skier transports. Some of them are equipped to carry skis on outside racks but require that snowboards be carried inside the car.

WARD OFF BOARD THEFT

All too common are the stories of snowboards being stolen while their owners are in the lodge getting some coffee or hot chocolate. Most ski resorts charge a nominal fee to store and guard your snowboard at *ski checks*—monitored corrals. If you really want to know where your snowboard is when you aren't riding, ski checks or locks are the way to go.

—Scott Downey

Don't leave your snowboard lying around unattended. Check it in at a ski corral to make sure it is safe. COURTESY TIMBERLINE SKI AREA

LIFT-LINE ENTRANCE SURVIVAL TIP

You need to stop and unbuckle or disengage your rear boot before entering a lift line. Protect yourself by stopping outside the flow of traffic and by facing uphill toward any oncoming skiers or boarders. Otherwise you're a sitting duck for a ski pole or board tip right into your back from the first speeding skier or out-of-control snowboarder to cross your path. Always be alert and avoid blocking the lift line while you are releasing the rear boot.

—*Charles Arnell*

Many resorts require you to place a protective sleeve (provided by the lift operator) over your snowboard when you carry it inside the car. This sleeve prevents the board from scratching the car's windows. Look ahead in line and watch how the snowboarders in front of you are doing things. If you have any questions, ask the lift operator before you attempt to enter the car.

Snow cats—tractor-powered machines that are usually used to groom slopes—provide another vehicle for taking snowboarders into otherwise inaccessible bowls.

The ultimate way to reach untracked snow is by helicopter. Helicopter boarding will provide some of the most gratifying turns for intermediate, advanced, and expert snowboarders. Helicopters can take you to some of the best, most exclusive snowboard terrain in the world—terrain that is accessible by no other means.

4 Let It Rip
Freeriding

OK. Here we are. You've mastered the chairlift and now you're on top of the hill. The ski lodge and lift lines are a quarter-mile and 800 vertical feet away. Somewhere in the back of your brain a little voice is shouting, "How am I ever going to get down there in one piece?!"

Simple. In this chapter we're going to learn to ride downhill at an easy, relaxed pace. We'll progress through some basic exercises to increase our edge control and feel for the fall line. Starting with sideslips and traverses, we'll go downhill slowly. Next, we'll practice garland turns one direction at a time. When you're ready, the big moment will come: we'll start linking together skidded turns in both directions.

By the time we leave this chapter, you'll be able to take off on your own and go *freeriding*. "What's freeriding?" you ask. Freeriding is taking off on any ol'

One of the world's top snowboarders, Mike Jacoby, freeriding at Treble Cone, New Zealand. TREVOR GRAVES

trail and doing what feels good. There are no judges, slalom gates, halfpipes, or clocks. You can carve the hard-pack or float through the powder, jump over bumps or bonk off stumps. Freeriding is a little bit of everything. Freeriding is *free* riding.

Warm-Up

Before we get started, let's loosen up again. Find a flat spot and buckle in. Stand up with a tall, relaxed stance and roll your board from edge to edge. Bend your knees and ankles a couple of times, and loosen up your arms. When you're ready to get started, take a look down the hill and find the fall line. Everything we're going to do in this chapter will center around the fall line.

Sideslipping

Think of sideslipping as skidding down the hill with the board perpendicular to the fall line and you'll have the picture. Sideslipping improves your balance and reinforces your edge control. It will also come in handy when you're peering down a slope too steep for your ability.

Practice sideslipping on your toe edge first since your toe and calf muscles are stronger and easier to control than heels and shins. Kneel uphill with your snowboard straight across the fall line and check to see if anyone's coming. Once the coast is clear, dig your toe edge into the snow and stand up equally balanced on the balls of both feet. (If you start sliding, tilt your board more to dig the

*To **sideslip** on your toe edge, balance on the balls of both feet and keep your snowboard straight across the fall line. Use your hands for balance and look up, not down. If you start to traverse in either direction, you can use your feet to steer your board back across the fall line.*

__Heelside sideslips__ are identical to toeside sideslips, except that you must balance on the heels of both feet.

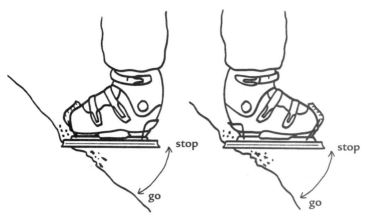

Sideslipping lets you skid downhill with the board perpendicular to the fall line. The harder you dig in the uphill edge, the slower you go. The flatter your board is to the snow, the faster you go. Be careful not to catch your downhill edge!

uphill edge into the snow. Let your knees and ankles do the tilting—don't just lean uphill.) Use your hands and arms for balance by holding them uphill in front of you. Now, peel your eyes away from your feet and look forward or slightly up the hill. Are you comfortable? Good, let's sideslip!

Straighten both knees a bit and gradually drop your heels. As the uphill edge lets go of the snow, your board will begin to slide downhill. *That's sideslipping!* Start slow at first, releasing just enough pressure on your toe edge to slide a few feet. Think about the pressures in your toes and calves. If you want to stop, firmly dig your toe edge in again. As you get more comfortable, increase the distance and speed of each sideslip. Whatever you do, don't let your heel edge catch during a sideslip. If you do, you will come to an abrupt halt as you slam backward onto the snow.

Try to make each sideslip smooth and even. *Listen* to your board and *look* at your tracks. Is your board brushing the snow in one smooth stroke or chopping it up like an ax? The smoother your sideslips, the better your control of the board. Also, control the board's direction with your feet. If one end slides downhill first, use your feet to steer your board back across the fall line. Remember, you're in control, not the board. You can steer the board back across the fall line with your feet.

When you're comfortable sideslipping on your toe edge—or if you just need a break—switch to your heel edge. This time, start from a seated position facing downhill, and stand up. (If you're having trouble standing up on a gentle slope, move to a slightly steeper hill. It's actually easier to dig your heel edge into steeper grades than it is on the flats.)

Now, do the same routine all over again. Keep a relaxed, upright stance, balance your weight evenly on your heels, and look up, not down. When you're ready, gradually drop your toes and start sideslipping. Be smooth, stay comfortably flexed, and resist the urge to dig in your heels. If you slam on the brakes or suddenly straighten your legs, you'll fall back on your butt or catch your toe edge and face-plant in the snow.

Traversing

Let's start at the top of the beginner slope again. This time, we're not going to slide *down* the hill, we're going to traverse *across* the hill. Traversing takes you from one side of the trail to the other in a gradual descent. By traversing back and forth, you can make it all the way down the mountain, tracing big Zs in the snow as you go. Snowboarding instructors call this zigzag path a *falling leaf*. In your first few days of snowboarding, traversing will get you down slopes that you are too timid to turn on. Later on, you can use traversing to get through tight spots, moguls, trees, and anything else that may intimidate you.

Traversing can be done on either edge, forward or fakie (backward). No matter which way you traverse, you do the same three things every time:

1. Look and face in the direction you want to go.
2. Shift more weight onto your leading foot.
3. *Steer* with your trailing foot.

Easy, right? Well, let's find out.

Heel-edge traverse, goofy foot.

Traversing *lets you ride from one side of a trail to the other in a gradual descent. Look in the direction you want to traverse, shift more weight onto your leading foot, and steer your board along its path using your trailing foot. If you get going too fast, push your back foot downhill and you'll slow down.*

1. Start of a **backward (fakie) heelside traverse** for a goofy-footed rider. Note that his head and hands are pointing in the direction of travel.

2. Nearing the end of the fakie heelside traverse and getting ready to change direction.

3. Starting a **heelside traverse** in the opposite direction. The rider is now riding **forward**, and his head and hands are shifting toward the new direction of travel.

4. Nearing the end of the forward heelside traverse.

5. The forward traverse has just ended and the rider is preparing for another fakie traverse.

6. With head and hands pointing forward, the rider is traversing fakie once again.

THE IMAGINARY BOX, PART ONE

An imaginary box can be used to improve everything from traverses to turns. To see how it works with traverses, try this: Start sideslipping on your toe edge. When you're ready to traverse, hold the imaginary box waist-high over the tip or tail and slide some weight onto the foot nearest the box. To begin traversing in that direction all you have to do is steer a little and stay on your uphill edge.

—*John Calkins, PSIA Instructor and Technical Director of High Cascade Snowboard Camp*

To start a toeside traverse, face uphill, stand on your toe edge, and begin a toeside sideslip. Once you're moving, look and turn your shoulders and hands toward the board's tip. At the same time, shift more of your weight onto your front foot. Your tip will drop down the hill a few inches and you'll start riding across the slope on your uphill edge. *That's traversing!*

Control your traverse in the same way you control your sideslips. Tilt the board up on its toe edge to traverse, or release the uphill edge to sideslip. The more you point your board down the fall line, the faster you'll go. If you're heading downhill too fast, push your back leg downhill to steer across the hill. If you want to go faster, put more weight on your front foot and look downhill. When it's time to stop, transfer more weight to your back leg and turn uphill. (Don't let the board turn too far uphill. Otherwise it will take off downhill again, backward!) Remember, *your front foot is the gas, and your back foot is the brake.*

Once you've finished a toeside traverse, you can traverse fakie on your toe edge, or sit down, turn around, and start a heelside traverse. To traverse fakie, look and turn your torso toward your tail and steer the tail downhill just a little. At the same

time shift more weight onto your back foot. Everything stays the same—you just do it all in reverse. Keep your weight toward the tail and steer with the leg nearest the tip.

Practice traversing every way you can: in both directions, on both edges, riding both forward and fakie. As you improve, mix short and long traverses together. Pretty soon, you'll be able to trace those falling leaves—without falling.

Garlands

When you can traverse forward in either direction, you're ready to work on some garland turns. (Don't worry if you can't ride fakie yet; that'll come with practice.) Garlands are series of skidded turns in one direction. They got their name from the path they leave in the snow, which looks like a garland draped on a Christmas tree. Garlands provide great

THE IMAGINARY BOX, PART TWO

The imaginary box is the ultimate tool for perfecting your turning skills. It teaches you to flex, extend, and control the pressure exerted on your edges during turns.

Pretend there are two shelves in front of you: a lower thigh-high shelf, and an upper chest-high shelf. At the start of each turn, sink into your snowboard by putting the box on the lower shelf. Toward the end of each turn, rise from your snowboard by lifting the box to the upper shelf. You will become more comfortable as your board arcs gently through each turn and releases smoothly between turns. This improves your control, makes turning easier, and lays the foundation for more advanced turns.

—*John Calkins, PSIA Instructor and Technical Director of High Cascade Snowboard Camp*

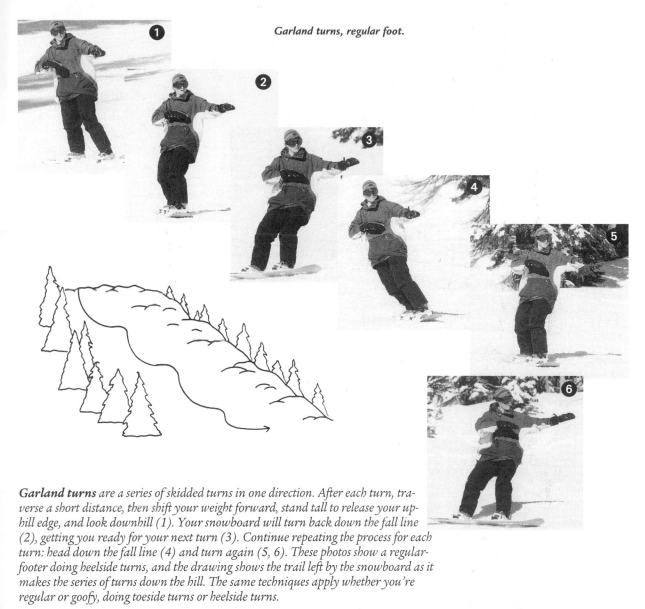

Garland turns, regular foot.

Garland turns are a series of skidded turns in one direction. After each turn, traverse a short distance, then shift your weight forward, stand tall to release your uphill edge, and look downhill (1). Your snowboard will turn back down the fall line (2), getting you ready for your next turn (3). Continue repeating the process for each turn: head down the fall line (4) and turn again (5, 6). These photos show a regular-footer doing heelside turns, and the drawing shows the trail left by the snowboard as it makes the series of turns down the hill. The same techniques apply whether you're regular or goofy, doing toeside turns or heelside turns.

turning practice without forcing you to link alternating toeside and heelside turns.

Let's start at the top of the hill again. Point the board down the fall line and begin a straight glide. Once you've got some speed going, begin a toeside turn. Since it has been a while since we've turned, let's go back over the basics. There are three main components of your turn: *looking* where you want to go, *weighting* your front foot, and *tilting* your board on its uphill edge. Finally, as the board begins to turn, sink slightly into the board by bending your knees and gently push your back leg downhill to steer.

As you finish your first turn and begin traversing across the hill on your uphill edge, get ready for your next turn. Transfer weight back to your front foot and flatten your board by relaxing your uphill edge. As the uphill edge (continued page 56)

Linked skidded turns—regular foot.

toeside

heelside

In making **linked turns,** riders always look where they want to go.
To link skidded turns, start down the fall line (1, both pages). Then go into a
skidded turn (2, both pages). Traverse a bit (3, both pages), then head downhill
again (4, both pages), before turning in the opposite direction and onto the other edge
(5 , 6, both pages).

Linked skidded turns—goofy foot.

toeside

① ② ③

heelside

④ ⑤ ⑥

(continued from page 53) begins to release, stand tall again—just like you did in a straight glide. Your board will turn downhill and drop down the fall line on another straight glide.

Keep repeating the process—turn, traverse, turn, traverse—until you reach the side of the trail. From there you can sit down, turn over, and do garland turns in the other direction. Practice garland turns in both directions, doing toeside turns in one direction, and heelside turns in the other.

Linked Skidded Turns

Take a minute to check out some snowboarders coming down a trail. They're probably not doing traverses or garlands. They're probably linking turns together and tracing beautiful Ss in the snow. Kind of makes you envious, huh? Well, no reason to be. With a little practice, you'll be linking turns too.

Think for a second how garlands worked. Starting from a straight glide, you looked in the direction you wanted to go, weighted your front foot, rolled onto your uphill edge, and steered with your feet. You sank into the board as it left the fall line, and evenly weighted your uphill edge to finish the traverse. When you were ready to begin a new turn, you extended your legs, released your uphill edge, and weighted your front foot. Your board turned back into the fall line, setting you up for your next turn.

Linked turns are like garlands, except that alternating toeside and heelside turns follow each straight glide (see photos pages 54–55).

Start with a tall, relaxed stance and drop into the fall line. Once you're moving, do a toeside or a heelside turn—whichever you like best. Traverse a little to get your bearings straight, then head down-

SLOW DOWN AND LEARN

The actual process of learning seems to occur at about half the speed you normally ride. If you find that incorrect technique is keeping you from advancing to the next performance level, slow down and practice proper techniques at half speed. Slower speeds give your mind time to think about what you are doing and your muscles a chance to build memory for the technique as well.

—*Charles Arnell*

hill again. (Look downhill, release your uphill edge, and shift your weight forward.) You're all set up to turn again. You just have to do it in the *opposite direction*. Relax and don't get onto the new edge too early. If you start turning too early, you'll catch your downhill edge and fall.

There, you just linked two turns together. Why don't you rest for a second and congratulate yourself? You're probably pretty excited, so take this opportunity to shake off the excess adrenaline. When you're calm again, try another set of linked turns, starting with the opposite turn first. Once you can turn toeside and heelside, you're ready to link turns all the way back to the lift line.

Speed Control

Remember the first time you did a straight glide? For some of you, feeling the board accelerate down

GOOD THINGS COME TO THOSE WHO WAIT

Linking skidded turns takes a bit of patience. As a beginner, it helps to wait until the board is unweighted and dropping down the fall line before you roll onto the opposite edge. If you begin your next turn before the board is pointed downhill, you'll catch the downhill edge and . . . *ouch*! As you improve, you can switch from one turn to another without having to point your board downhill first.

—*Scott Downey*

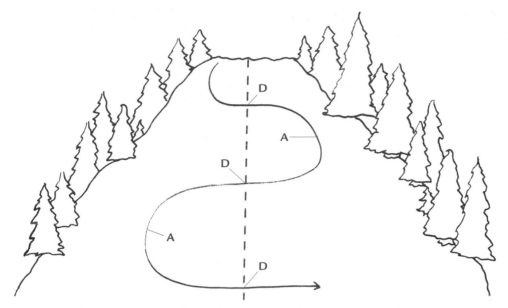

One of the keys to controlling your speed is understanding how to use the fall line. As you begin to drop down the fall line (riding downhill), your snowboard accelerates. You can slow down by turning back across the fall line (across the hill). In this diagram, the As show where you'll accelerate, and the Ds show where you'll decelerate.

the fall line was intimidating. Now that you're in control of your snowboard, you can turn or traverse at will. The only time you pick up speed is when you're actually heading downhill.

Think about that for a second: The only time you pick up speed is when you're actually heading downhill. Every time you turn, you leave the fall line and traverse across the hill. If you're going faster and faster with each successive turn, it's because you're spending more time *in* the fall line than *across* the fall line. In other words, you're not finishing your turns.

One way to check your speed is to finish each turn so that your board is going across—not down—the slope. You can also slow your descent by pressuring your uphill edge earlier in your turns and working on the shape of your turns. Smooth, round, continuous S-turns are the way to go.

Refinements

Flexing and Extending

Try turning your board with your legs totally straight. Doesn't work, does it? How about if you're squatting all the way down—can you turn now? No way! Your legs power and guide your skidded turns, so let's learn how to get the most out of them.

You've already learned a little bit about how *sinking into* and *rising out of* your turns improves them. (This is called *weighting* and *unweighting* by many instructors.) Now we're going to spend more time concentrating on these vertical movements to get us ready for carved turns.

Let's start with a straight glide and proceed into a toeside or heelside turn. As you start your turn, flex your knees and ankles, letting your whole body sink into the board. Don't bend at your waist. Sink with your knees. Do this all the way through the end of the turn, feeling your board flex under your feet. (This is the weighting phase.) As you cross the hill, rise and extend your legs to help release the board from the snow and make it easier to drop back down the fall line. (This is the unweighting phase.)

Practice sinking and rising through every turn. Do it slowly on wide turns and quickly on narrow turns. Practice sinking and rising at different

extended ❶

flexed ❷

flexed ❸

MIDGETS AND GIANTS

Are you having trouble understanding sinking and rising motions? Try this:

Become a *midget* as you're turning and traversing across the hill. Get low by bending your knees and ankles, but keep your head up and back straight.

As you end one turn and get ready for the next, become a *giant*. Stand up as tall as you can, and let the board drop into the fall line. As you begin your next turn, become a midget again and repeat the process.

By practicing these overexaggerated sinking and rising movements, you'll quickly become more comfortable flexing and extending your legs during turns.

—*Hillary Maybery, 1992 U.S. Amateur Snowboarding Association (USASA) National Champion*

speeds until you can feel the board grab the snow to support you during turns and release easily between turns.

Timing Your Turns

Learning to time your turns helps develop rhythmic movements and correct body positions. Timing improves the flow of your riding and helps you figure out whether your technique is correct. If your technique is good, you will take the same amount of time to initiate both toeside and heelside turns.

Timing turns is simple. Before you start a run, decide what count you would like to give each turn. For example, start with turns that take a five-count. (I picked five because it is easy to count to and gives a nice medium-range turn.) As soon as you initiate the first turn, begin counting—*one, two, three, four, five*—while you are on an edge. At the end of the five-count, immediately initiate your next turn on the opposite edge. Count again—*one, two, three, four,*

extended

④

⑤

Sinking into your turns and rising out of your turns (sometimes called weighting *and* unweighting *your snowboard) will improve your control and confidence. As you start turning, sinking helps flex the board and puts the sidecut into closer contact with the snow. Sinking also puts you into a more athletic stance that lets you adjust to changes in the terrain. Rising—or extending—out of your turns releases your uphill edge and makes it easier to turn your board back down the fall line. Try sinking and rising at different speeds and under a variety of conditions to find what works best for you.*

five—while you are on that edge, and turn again at the end of the five-count.

Training yourself to turn on a particular count challenges your body to stay engaged in the turns—to round each one out, release your edge, extend upward, and immediately reengage the opposite edge. There's no slop, skidding, or waiting for the right time to turn. If you find that the rhythms of your toeside and heelside turns are different, go back and study your technique. Look at your body position again, and commit to timing

each turn. You'll see improvements in your technique right away.

Using the Upper Body

Your upper body is just as important as your legs in snowboarding. If your head and shoulders are turning left while your board and feet are turning right, you've got big problems. Let's divide the upper body into two sections and figure out what to do with each.

STAY LOOSE

Snowboarding is a dynamic, flowing sport. You need to be able to adapt to the snow and terrain as you ride. One of the keys to efficient snowboarding is staying relaxed and comfortable. A great way to accomplish this is to take a few re-laxation breaths—slow and deep from the abdomen—before each run. It's also a great idea to shake out your major muscle groups before each run. Once you're riding, stay loose and feel what your body is doing. You'll have a lot more fun!

—*Lowell Hart, Professional Ski Instructors of America Snowboard Education Team*

Whether you're riding straight or turning, keep your hands level, with your arms comfortably spread in front of you.

The first upper-body section consists of your *head* and *back*. They provide a lot of balance in snowboarding. To keep that balance going, you have to keep your back and head up. Think about that for a second. When you first started snowboarding, you spent a fair amount of time bending over and looking at the ground. And when you did that, you fell. Right? The more you look down at the snow, the more likely you are to fall into it.

Your *arms* are the second most important part of the upper body. The arms can make up 10 to 15 percent of upper-body weight, so if they're out of control, they're probably throwing you off balance.

Your arms should be comfortably flexed and slightly out in front of you. Starting from this neutral, balanced position, you're ready to turn. Many contemporary instructors have students keep their hands and arms in this open, level position throughout the turn to keep them balanced. If you can imagine a tightrope walker using the arms for balance, you'll understand this concept.

A few instructors, however, allow the front hand to cross from one edge of the board to the other in order to help weight one edge at a time. Think of it this way: if you're going to do a toeside turn, pretend your front hand is bouncing a basketball over your toe edge. On heelside turns, bounce that same bas-

ketball back over your heel edge. This simple drill *closes* your shoulders on toeside turns and *opens* your shoulders on heelside turns.

Though the balanced-arm approach is more the norm these days, don't rule out any style of riding until you try it first.

Practice

You now have the tools to ride a wide variety of terrain. You can take your newfound skills from beginner trails on up to intermediate slopes or beyond. Still, you should practice everything you've learned. Being able to do everything well—turning, traversing, walking—will keep you smiling all day long and fuel your desire to stay on the snowboard. When you've mastered everything up to this point, you're ready to begin carving your turns and getting ready for the advanced techniques discussed in chapter 5.

Carved Turns

In chapter 2 we talked about three ways to turn a snowboard: *skidded turns*, *carved turns*, and *jump turns*. Up to now, skidded turns have worked just fine. They've taught you the basics of edge control and weight placement, but they're also pretty noisy and sloppy.

Now it's time to graduate to carved turns. Carved turns eliminate most of your back leg's steering movements, they drive your upper body through the turn, and they let the board do what it is designed to do. Instead of skidding across the surface of the snow, the board arcs under your feet as the edges slice through the snow. The board's sidecut and flex supply the turning power, while you provide edge control and weight shifts. The net result is a clean, narrow, round track that looks awesome and feels great.

Before we practice carved turns, let's go back to traverses and garlands on the bunny slope. Remember what it felt like the first time you did a traverse? Your board skidded around, leaving in its snowy wake a chaotic path of slits, scrapes, and ridges. Now that you've developed a keen feel for

Rider Mark Fawcett slices through a carved turn on Blackcomb Glacier, British Columbia.
DANO PENDYGRASSE

your edges, try traversing without skidding at all. You'll have to flex your knees and ankles more, and rock the board up higher on edge to make this work, but you can do it!

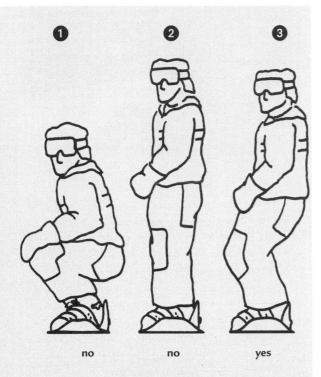

50/50

Snow conditions and terrain change constantly. Riding with your knees slightly bent will help you absorb bumps and reach into hollows to keep you riding smoothly.

Check out the drawings here. Rider #1 is squatting as far down as possible. If a bump comes along, what's he going to do? He can't bend his knees any more, so he's going to fall. Rider #2 is standing totally tall. If he passes over a hollow, he can't extend his legs, so he'll fall too. Rider #3 is ready for everything. He can flex his legs 50 percent for the bumps and 50 percent for the hollows. Snowboarding coaches call this the 50/50 position. That's the way *you* want to ride out on the hill.

—*Scott Downey*

After a couple of traverses, try some garlands. Last time you were doing garlands, you skidded your turns by steering with your feet. Now it's time to let the edges turn the board for you. (Remember all that talk about sidecut and turning radius in chapter 2? Here's where it comes into play.)

Start your first garland the same as you did before—dropping straight down the fall line, then looking, weighting, and tilting as always. This time, however, get on your edge earlier in your turn and roll your knees and hips to the inside of the turn. Keep your upper body tall and your hands level, but increase the flex in your knees and ankles to tilt the board higher on edge.

One good way to visualize what your knees are supposed to do is to think of your back knee driving toward the toe edge on toeside turns, and toward the heel edge on heelside turns. Some riders describe this as pointing your knees in the direction of your turn. You can do the same thing with your feet. Think of your toes pointing in the direction you want to turn, and feel your feet pressure the sides of your boot bladders. All of these concepts sound pretty strange when you read about them, but they really work when you use them on the slopes.

One thing you must do to carve turns is to flex the camber out of the snowboard. By keeping your *knees closer together* and sinking more aggressively than you did in skidded turns, you'll put more pressure on the middle of the board and help it flex into the arc of the turn.

You should *hear*, *see*, and *feel* a difference between carved turns and skidded turns. Telltale scraping sounds will let you know that your snowboard is skidding. Carved turns, on the other hand, will be much quieter. Narrow, neat tracks will curve behind you if you're carving, while broad, messy tracks will let you know you need more practice. Finally, you'll feel more precision and power when you're carving turns. Once you get that feeling, you'll seek it every time you're out on the groomed slopes.

Getting Better

You've learned many new techniques in this chapter. Just a little while ago you were struggling with

EDGE AWARENESS

When you're riding fast on a flat base, you're in *no man's land*—a place where either edge can take control without warning. As you glide along, little imperfections in the snow kick your board around. If the downhill edge suddenly catches while your board is shimmying across the snow, you'll fall.

Now that you've become comfortable with both edges, spend more of your time on them. Pressure one edge or the other, even when you aren't turning. You don't have to crank the board up on edge, just weight one edge (usually the uphill edge) slightly. This will lock your board into the snow and keep it on a predictable, stable path.

—David Sher, 1991 California State All Around Master's Champion

garlands. Now you're linking carved turns. Still, people are tossing tips at you faster than you can digest them. If you're like me, it's impossible to make sense of so much new information when you're trying to improve one skill at a time.

Instead of memorizing everything you've learned about turning in this chapter, remember these five important tips:

1. Look in the direction you want to go. Wherever your head goes, your body follows.

2. Keep your weight forward. Not all the time, but most of the time. If you're out of control, shift your weight forward and you'll probably avoid a fall.

3. Keep your knees bent. If you're washing out on heelside turns, bend your knees. You'll be amazed how much it improves your control.

4. Maintain a tall upper body. This will keep you upright and balanced in almost any situation.

5. Avoid twisting or pivoting too much when you're turning. Instead, flex and extend with your knees to get your board to carve and release each turn.

Take these tips out on the hill and practice some more. Every once in a while test yourself. Is your upper body tall? Are you looking in the direction of each turn? Are you keeping your knees bent? If you answer *yes* to each of these questions, you're ready to move on to chapter 5. If you answer *no*, keep practicing. Proceed at your own pace, and just have fun!

5 Crank It Up
Alpine Riding

Charles Arnell ripping through some light crust in the back-country of Aspen, Colorado. JOHN BING

When snowboarding was in its infancy, riders strapped their feet to wooden boards with bungee cords, stood sideways, and swiveled their feet to turn. Control was something experienced by only the most athletic snowboarders, and some snow conditions were simply impossible to ride. Metal edges and sidecut changed all of that, making carved turns as easy for snowboarders as they are for skiers.

In this chapter we'll perfect our carving skills and push freeriding to its limits. Our carved turns will look cool, feel good, and work great in almost any type of snow or terrain. We'll prove that by learning to ride moguls, powder, and ice. By the end of this chapter we'll be able to handle anything the mountain can dish out—trees, crud, steeps, jumps—*anything!*

Techno-Carving

Why Techno-Carve?

If we had to divide snowboarders into just two camps, freestyle riders would be on one side, and alpine riders and racers would be on the other. While most freestylers are riding soft boots and angling their stances *across* their boards, most alpine riders and racers are riding hard boots and angling their stances *up* their boards. While both camps use the same basic skills to turn, freestylers' sideways stances require more body rotation to turn than racers' stances do.

The racers' steep foot angles put their upper bodies into a *square stance*—a stance where their hips and shoulders are more perpendicular to the long axis of their board. From this stance, a quiet upper body complements the lower body to produce smooth, fast, carved turns. We'll call these technically precise turns *techno-carve turns*.

Everybody can benefit from the racers' techno-carving techniques, especially *freeriders* and *alpine riders*. For example, a lot of snowboarders lean their upper body into their turns and fall when their board *sketches* out from under them. When you're techno-carving, you are perfectly balanced over your board's carving edge, so you'll still be standing if the board begins to slip out of a turn. Sound too good to be true? Well, let's see how it works.

Techno-Carving Techniques

Before you can techno-carve, you've got to set your body stance and get your board moving. Stand in a good racing position. Your knees should be slightly flexed (just like in the 50/50 sidebar on page 54) and your arms should be in the *outrigger* position (hands forward, just above your hips, and slightly wider than your shoulders). Once you're set, start gliding down the fall line. When you've gained enough speed to make your first turn, you can begin to techno-carve.

To make techno-carving easy to understand, we've broken it down into six steps. These steps

By turning their foot angles forward, racers are able to keep their hips and shoulders more perpendicular to the long axis of their snowboards. This stance can make carving a lot easier. TREVOR GRAVES

blend together when you're riding, but they can be practiced separately if you think about them. Here they are:

1. *Look* in the direction you want to go. (Whichever way your head looks, your body follows!)

2. *Drive* your knees and back hand into the turn.

3. *Keep* a tall upper body all the way through the turn. (Three tricks to make that happen: First, pinch your outside hipbone and ribs together in the turn to keep your upper body and back *straight*. Second, pretend that a carpenter has hung a *plumb line* down the middle of your forehead; keep that line between your eyes, down through the middle of your chest, and through your belly button. Third, keep your shoul-

A high-speed techno-carved turn allows Charles Arnell's lower body to extend outward while his upper body remains upright and balanced.

ders and hands *aligned* with the slope of the hill and in front of your body.)

4. *Sink* progressively faster into the turn.
5. *Rise* progressively faster out of the turn.
6. *Look* in the new direction you want to go and start your next turn.

Techno-Carving Exercises

Professional coaches have come up with some great drills to reinforce the mechanics of techno-carved turns. At many racing camps (the *only* place where you can try this first drill), coaches have their riders hold a long bamboo pole level in front of their bodies, hands at least shoulder width apart. The trick is to keep the pole level so that neither end drags in the snow. The more level the pole, the more *plumb* and *level* the rider's upper body. To work the *pinch*, students hold the pole behind their neck on top of their shoulders. (The pole is held with the hands so that it can be released during a fall; draping your arms over the pole invites shoulder dislocations.) In that position, the only way you can keep the pole level in a turn is to pinch your outside hip and rib together.

Pinching *your outside hipbone and ribs together during turns helps keep your upper body tall and your back straight. This snowboarder is making a toeside turn to his left, so he's pinching his right hipbone and ribs together.*

A tall upper body helps keep you balanced over your carving edge. Two tricks help keep your upper body tall. First, keep your hands aligned with the slope of the hill. (This rider's hand positions are exaggerated. You may wish to keep your hands more in front of your body.) Second, pretend that a carpenter has hung a plumb line through your forehead, chest, and belly button. Use that imaginary line to keep your upper body tall.

Another good exercise is called *grab-carving*. Grab-carving helps students grasp the pinch, plumb, and level concepts without carrying around any extra devices. To grab-carve, grab the board's outside edge with the outside hand while riding the inside carving edge. (If you can't grab it, just touch it with your fingers for now.) Make your ankles and knees do all the work, and keep your back straight. Your upper body will stay vertical, and your hipbone will pinch against your rib. Since the board will accelerate every time you slice a new turn, it'll take a while before you get used to the speed. When you can link four or five grab-carves in a row without falling, you're getting it!

To keep improving, start techno-carving steeper slopes at higher speeds, and through a variety of terrain and snow conditions. When you feel comfortable techno-carving intermediate or advanced runs, you may be ready to test your skills on the race course.

Eurocarving

While the racers are concentrating on techno-carving, a handful of wild freeriders and alpine riders are out on the groomed trails laying their board high on an edge and diving into one of snowboarding's most exciting turns—*Eurocarve turns*.

Eurocarve turns are just the opposite of techno-carve turns. Instead of being upright, your upper body is laid out on the snow. Instead of balancing over your board, you're diving into the turn. Eurocarving takes a lot of speed and commitment, but the payoff is a huge adrenaline rush.

To Eurocarve, start off with a lot of speed and shoot for a medium- or large-radius turn on well-groomed, soft-packed snow. As you start the turn, get low and be powerful. Reach all the way into the inside of the turn with your inside hand, and crank the board as high on edge as it'll go.

As you lay your body across the snow, you've got to balance everything together—centrifugal force, board angle, body angle—to keep the board from sketching. If you do sketch or fall, you don't have far to go—you're already on the snow. You might, however, end up with a wad of snow stuffed up your jacket!

Be sure the area around you is clear before you begin to wildly rail on your edge, since traffic above you may not anticipate your turns across the fall line.

Handling Different Types of Snow

What's your favorite kind of snow? Bottomless powder, groomed soft-pack, spring corn? Now, what type of snow do you usually ride? Sierra cement, Cascade concrete, Appalachian ice? If we really thought about it, we could probably come up with dozens of names for different types of snow conditions. Just think how hard snowboarding would be if each type of snow demanded a different technique. It would be enough to make you want to stay home.

Takeuchi grab-carves at Val Thorens, France. GALLUP

CARVING AND RACING

To improve your carving and racing skills, first go out and carve a variety of turns on a lot of different terrain until you're used to making any type of turn. Next, break down your turns into different parts so that you can improve each part gradually. Concentrate on balancing over your board, even if it slips out during a turn; use your knees to initiate turns, pressing on your toes and heels to make your board carve; and keep your upper body as tall and as quiet as you can.

As your basic turning skills improve, things like timing and use of the fall line will fall into place. As you improve, keep coming back to work on every element of your turns. You should see your times get faster and faster.

—Mike Jacoby, 1991
Overall World Champion;
1st Place Giant Slalom 1992 World Cup

Fortunately, all types of snow conditions can be ridden with similar techniques. Granted, each type of snow has a slightly different feel, but each takes only a little fine-tuning of skills you already have. Once you're comfortable with the little tricks in this section, you can pick out the best available snow on any particular day and ride it. When the bumps are frozen solid, you can move onto groomed runs and carve. When the groomed trails get boring, you can head into the back bowls and ride the powder. There are all kinds of riding opportunities on the mountain. This section is your introduction to them.

Powder

Many snowboarders consider powder to be the ultimate in weightless pleasure. Powder is surfing. Powder is floating. Powder can melt the distinction between ground and sky and send your board flying effortlessly through space.

For all of its magic, powder sometimes intimidates the unfamiliar rider. Maybe those fears come from the fact that beginners can't learn by watching another rider's snowboard as it *porpoises* or *banks* because it is veiled in a cloud of frozen crystals. Whatever the source of these fears, powder is no problem once you fine-tune your freeriding techniques.

Riding powder is not very different from the kind of boarding you already know how to do. Powder is, after all, *just snow!* It's a little deeper and lighter than your average snow, but that just means you'll bog down if you go too slowly or have a trickier time standing up after falls. Other than that, the skills we discuss here will make powder some of the best snow you can ride.

The first key to riding powder is *speed*. Think of a water skier being dragged behind a powerboat: it takes some speed before the skis plane to the surface and lift the skier above the water. The same thing happens when you're snowboarding. If you go slow, you sink. Once that happens, the snow wraps around your legs and drags you to a halt. Speed lets you plane.

Pick an open, unobstructed slope for your first powder run. Point your board straight down the

Pietro Colturi lays out a big Eurocarve turn at Passo Stelvio. FLUCIS

Charles Arnell in chest-deep powder in British Columbia. JOHN KELLY

fall line and let it rip! Forget about your edges for a minute, and ride the base flat. If your board dives when you're riding, slide your center of mass back a few inches toward the tail. Sitting back a bit can help keep the tip up and planing. Once your board begins to float, *bounce gently* a couple of times. Let your *knees* do the work while your upper body

floats along. Feel how this makes your board float and dive like a porpoise playing in the ocean. That *porpoising* action will become part of your turns in a minute.

It only takes a little effort to turn in powder. As you come to the top of a bounce (like a porpoise coming up for air), steer and turn in a new direc-

SAFETY IN POWDER

Powder can be the ultimate downhill thrill! However, nonreleasable snowboard bindings can also make powder dangerous. The following safety tips will keep your trips safe and enjoyable.

1. Never snowboard alone. Make sure you can see and hear your fellow riders.
2. Keep up your speed to avoid bogging down. Avoid flat areas and long traverses.
3. Learn to stand up in a small patch of powder near a groomed slope, and practice frog-hopping to firmer snow.
4. Avoid hidden traps like tree wells, rocks, and stumps.
5. Avoid slopes prone to avalanches and slough slides. Consider carrying a two-way radio with you so you can call for help if you get stuck.

—Scott Downey

tion. Don't let the board slow or stall. Instead, before you begin to slow down, let your board sink back down into the fall line, bounce again, and turn the other way.

You only have to tilt slightly from one edge to the other to make your first powder turns. Once you're comfortable *banking* off light snow, you can increase your time on each edge. Let your turns flow with a natural porpoising rhythm. Rise, steer, rise, steer, rise, steer. The beat will be addicting!

Ice

Few snowboarders like riding on ice. It magnifies your mistakes and saps your confidence. Fortunately, most ice isn't really *ice*, it's just hard snow—old white stuff that's been packed solid or thawed by the sun and refrozen at night. It'll hold an edge, but not all that well. In this section, if the snow is hard enough to make edging difficult, we'll call it ice. If edging is impossible, we'll call it quits.

Before you try snowboarding ice, sharpen your edges as described in chapter 10, or have them sharpened at your local board shop. Most modern snowboards will slice and hold an edge on the hardest surfaces if the edges are well tuned and polished. Also, carry a small whetstone to keep your edges sharp all day.

Next, make sure you're locked tight to your board. Clamp down your highback bindings tight to secure your feet, or consider using hard boots. Whatever kind of boots you use, get rid of the slop. The tiniest bit of play between your feet, boots, and board will be exaggerated when you try to hold a turn. Finally, think about wearing knee pads and wrist guards. (If you're worried about your buddies laughing, just hide them under your clothes and know who'll have the last laugh.) Once you've got everything put together you're ready to slice the ice.

For your first ice ride, do a *check turn*—a short turn quickly followed by some hard-edged sideslipping. The check turn will bolster your confidence and allow you to move on to carved turns. Once you've got your balance down and nerves under control, you're ready to carve.

Smooth, subtle, continuous turns are the key to snowboarding ice. If you ram your weight into the board or overload an edge, it'll sketch out from under you. The only way to go is to ride delicately and to listen to your edges. If you start chattering, turn! Don't hang on a traverse too long—keep carving.

Finally, always keep an eye on the snow in front of you. There's less friction between your snowboard and ice than there is between your snowboard and soft snow. So if you fly across the ice into a patch of softer snow, you'll lunge forward as the snow puts on the brakes. When you move from snow to ice, your board will want to take off in front of you and drop you on your butt. Anticipation is the key to riding mixed snow conditions. Look where you're going, and you'll see what you need to do.

Crust and Crud

Think of *crust* as a fruit pie. It's soft in the middle and crusty on top. When snowboarders are

Tom Burt blasts through the crud. JOHN KELLY, COURTESY KEMPER SNOWBOARDS

talking about crust, they're describing soft snow that's covered by a hard layer of snow. When your board sinks into the softer layer, the crust batters your shins and makes snowboarding difficult.

Solid crust is almost impossible to ride. It buries your board and sends you cartwheeling forward. Still, lots of crust can be ridden if you're positive and precise. The key is to be aggressive in order to get the board out of the snow to make your turns. To do that, use more upward extension after each turn to break your snowboard free of the snow, then pull your knees up to turn the board in the air. Once the board is turned, flex your legs to push it back into the snow and finish your turn.

Think of *crud* as disassembled igloo blocks or big chunks of Styrofoam. Crud can be heavy, broken-up powder, or tracked-up soft-pack. It often appears after a few skiers or snowboarders have sliced up thick blocks of dense snow, leaving the slope broken and irregular.

Ride crud the same way you ride crust. Pull your knees up to free your board from the snow and make your turns in the air. Keep your turns short and bouncy. Be aggressive and attack the fall line. Most of all, keep your knees bent and your legs ready to flex or extend to compensate for ruts and bumps.

CRUD

Thick, chunky, tracked-up blocks of crud snow can challenge any snowboarder. Still, riding crud is a lot more fun than its cruddy name implies. It just takes a little practice and a couple of technique refinements. Besides being aggressive and rhythmic, you can employ a few tactics used by top snowboarders to make this type of snow easier to ride.

1. Always look ahead to find the best line.
2. Use small piles of snow as small jumps to launch you over large blocks of snow.
3. Vary the radius of your turns to avoid the biggest piles of dense snow.
4. If you're going to ride through a dense pile of snow, sit back a bit so you don't get catapulted forward.

Ultimately you want to stick with your game plan and not get psyched out. Even if your friends look like they can ride crud with ease, they're getting jarred and jolted just like you. The key to having fun in the crud is to minimize the jostling by maximizing your power and control.

—*Scott Downey*

Handling Varied Terrain
Moguls

Picture your common mogul field: a parking lot of VW Beetles, buried in three feet of snow, tilted at a 30-degree angle. If you're like me, you feel like a running back about to bounce off 487 linebackers. If you're a lot better than me, that mogul field signals *fun!* No matter who you are, there's always room to improve your mogul techniques.

There are many ways to approach moguls. You can traverse across the fall line, turn in the troughs, or turn on the tops of the bumps. As your expertise grows, you can ride moguls however you want, but for now you're probably just trying to find a way to get down mogul fields intact. Emerging at the bottom of a mogul field in one piece starts with good techniques that can be learned one mogul at a time.

Your first mogul run should be on a small, gently tilted slope. Pick a short downhill line through a couple of bumps and get psyched to ride them. If the hill is too steep or you're too scared to drop down the fall line, just pick a tree slightly downhill on the far side of the mogul field for your goal. The line you take through the moguls will traverse the slope and end up at that tree.

Approach your first bump slowly and drive your back hand forward to get in a powerful, aggressive stance. Absorb the front and top of the bump with your knees, then extend your legs to push the tip down the back of the mogul into the trough. While your lower body bounces like a spring, your head just floats along level—like a car on shock absorbers. By floating your head and sucking up the bumps with your knees, you maintain your balance and keep your vision clear.

After your first couple of bumps, you can begin turning. Stop at the top of a bump and look at your board. The tip and tail are hanging out there in the air, totally unweighting and just begging to be turned. Go for it! Turn your board on the top of one bump, then try it again on the next few bumps. Absorb the bumps with your knees, turn in a new direction on the tops of the bumps, and extend your legs to push the board back into the troughs. Absorb the bumps, turn the board, extend in the troughs. Absorb, turn, extend. Remember to float your head.

While some riders try to make all of their turns on top of the bumps, this is very difficult for most riders. Try your next few turns in the troughs as if you were making small-radius turns on a groomed slope. The moguls will force you to vary your path frequently, but that's where looking ahead and planning come into play.

Once you've mastered basic bump moves, you can begin to make your rides flow. Start to plan your ride three to five turns ahead. Look at the

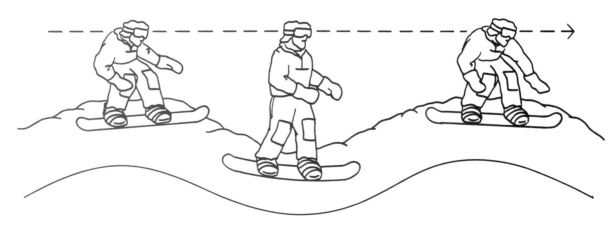

When riding moguls, drive your back hand forward, keep your head level, and let your legs absorb the bumps like giant springs.

downhill side of the bumps and decide whether you're going to follow the fall line or turn across the slope to slow your descent. Mix up fast, steep turns with slower, tighter turns to keep the pace smooth and comfortable. If you have trouble after the second or third turn into the mogul field, this indicates that your toeside or heelside turning techniques are off. Look back to the Refinements section in chapter 4 and see if you can adjust your turning techniques until these problems disappear. Work up to the point that you can attack the entire mogul field nonstop, then try something a little steeper. Challenge yourself to keep improving.

Steeps

When you were first learning to snowboard, the bunny slopes seemed steep. Later on, intermediate glades seemed steep. Now we're beyond all that. Now we're talking black-diamond steep. Pitches that force you to put everything you've learned together.

There are two basic ways to ride the steeps: aggressively or conservatively. Back in chapter 4, you learned that sideslips can be used to bail you out

How steep is steep? Josh Heminger finds some big vertical during a helicopter outing in British Columbia. JOHN KELLY

MOGULS

Your back hand is a good indicator of your mogul technique. It will want to drift and flail behind you. Once it's back there, it will throw you into the back seat, off balance, and onto your butt. Drive your back hand forward in the moguls. If it falls behind you, pull it forward and put it back in front of you. This keeps you in an aggressive, balanced stance, and makes moguls easier to ride.

—*Scott Downey*

Matt Cummins drops into a giant mogul field in Aspen, Colorado. TREVOR GRAVES

of trouble on steep slopes. If you're in trouble now, sideslipping may be an option. Sideslipping steeps may even make you comfortable enough to try them—some other day. That's because the more time you hang out in scary places, the safer they seem to become.

If you're standing at the top of a steep slope confident and poised, drop in and turn. In fact, *jump turn*. Jump turns take compression and extension to new heights. You jump to unweight your board, pivot in the air, then land on the opposite edge.

You don't have to learn jump turns on the side of a towering 50-degree slope. You can practice them on a steep bank amidst gentler slopes. Start from a good platform. Stand on your uphill edge with your body leaning away from the hill and your shoulders straight across the fall line. When you're ready to turn, look and steer into the turn with your shoulders, hop up to turn, then land straight across the fall line again. (As always, look in the direction of each turn.) The net result is usually a controlled skidded turn. Whatever it is, end up on another balanced platform and stay alert for buried ice or slough snow so you can sideslip or turn again in a hurry.

As you practice jump-turning, focus on these specifics:

1. Visualize your descent before you take the plunge. Know exactly where you are going to make your first turn and visualize how you're going to do it.
2. Set a comfortable cadence once you start turning and keep it going.
3. Be aggressive and positive, and concentrate on your turns.
4. Anticipate changes in the snow so your board doesn't catch or slide out from under you.

The more you think about what you're doing, the less chance there is for negative thoughts to sabotage your success. When you've grown accustomed to short, steep slopes, you can take your newfound skills to taller trails.

Chutes

Chutes—narrow passages down the mountain—can be steep or moderate, soft or icy. You can usually handle them like any other terrain, except that your options will be more limited.

Freeriding gentler slopes strewn with obstacles provides great practice for chutes. Take off into boulder fields, trees, brush—anything that will force you to turn. Being able to turn anywhere, and at any time, will provide the skills and the confidence you need to maneuver in tight spots.

If you haven't run a particular chute before, scout it out ahead of time and plan your descent. If you don't know how to recognize avalanche hazards, avoid the chute altogether or defer to the knowledge of an avalanche expert.

Once you have determined that the chute is safe to ride, visualize each turn and where you want your board to be. You may be able to carve turns in the widest parts of the chute, then have to resort to a couple of sideslips or jump turns to clear the crux. Don't let the chute psych you out. Know where you want to go, how you're going to do it, then do it. Don't hesitate! He who hesitates . . . falls.

Jumps

Your first jump has already happened. You remember the scene—you hit a bump with stiff knees, and *kaboing!* You were airborne. Chances are you crashed, too. Right? Then why is catching air so addicting? Because once you learn to jump, you're able to fly at will. Toy with gravity. Test your limits. After all, to air is human.

The first part of jumping is figuring out what a jump is. Basically, you can jump anywhere you want—within reason. Hopping on the flats is jumping. Hitting a bump and launching a foot or two off the ground is jumping. For now, we'll talk about big bumps and small dropoffs. Find something with a two- to five-foot drop, a clean approach, and a clean landing. (Scout out locations ahead of time.)

For your first jump, hit the lip straight with barely enough speed to catch some air. Start low

Learn to jump on small jumps first, then move on to gradually larger jumps as you begin to feel more comfortable. Draw your knees up and keep everything level during the jump to stay balanced and ready for a safe landing. PHOTO OF DAVE COLLIER BY JONNY BEALL, WISHBONE IMAGES

and compressed with your weight centered over your board. Your back should be straight, your head up, and your arms out in front of you for balance. Finish up your turns ahead of time so that you hit the jump square, then flatten the board just before takeoff.

The jump itself will be easy: jump with both feet, enjoy the flight, and land on both feet. When you get to the lip, jump straight up or just ride off it. As your front foot clears the lip, lift it up. Once you're in the air, draw both knees up to level out the board and stay compressed. Keep your head up, your back straight, and your arms quiet. Looking at the landing will keep you from wobbling off-center and will get you ready for the touchdown.

WHEN IN DOUBT, AIR IT OUT

Knowing how to jump can tremendously improve your overall riding technique. Air awareness gives you the confidence to charge down hills, cut across cat tracks, and launch off of lips. And if you ever speed down a hill, over a knoll, and suddenly find that the ground drops out from beneath you, air awareness increases your chances of landing upright big time! Think like a cat, and always try to land on your feet.

—*Charles Arnell*

This photo is for entertainment purposes only. Few riders in the world would ever dare to jump cliffs like this one. PHOTO OF MATT GOODWILL BY LONNIE BALL, MONTANA POWDER GUIDES

ROLLING DOWN THE WINDOW

A lot of riders lose control of their arms in jumps while concentrating on straight backs, level boards, and proper weight distribution. Once they're slightly off balance, airborne riders **roll down the window**—throw their arms around in big circles—in a futile attempt to keep their body upright. Since arms make up about 10 to 15 percent of your body weight, they can easily throw you off balance when they're swinging wildly. Rolling down the window can cause you to sit back on the board or go over the tip.

Keep your arms quiet on your next jump. Put them in front of you for balance, and use them to guide you toward your landing. You should see the benefits right away.

—J. D. Platt, 11th overall World Cup and 4th place Halfpipe in the Professional Snowboarders Association (PSA) of North America

Reach for the landing with your legs like a plane dropping its landing gear and suck it up by bending deep at your knees. The key here is to touch down quietly with both feet at the same time. If the snow is too soft or deep to make that work, lean back a bit, then readjust after you land. Since you'll be going fast when you hit, get ready to turn to check your speed. (For many riders, it's easier to turn toeside after a jump; that's because your calf muscles are stronger and easier to control.) On the other hand, never try to land on your toe or heel edge. If you do, your foot could be painfully crushed into the end of your boot.

Perfect the small jumps before you start to go bigger. Practice, practice, practice! If you're going too fast into a jump, you can slow down by scrubbing some speed. Scrub speed by kicking your back foot out like you would with a skidded turn, then straightening your board back up for the jump. If

you're falling on your butt or on your hands and knees, look at your takeoff: if you're jumping from your toe edge, you'll land on your knees. If you're jumping from your heel edge, you'll land on your butt. Jump from a *flat base* by kicking the tail out a bit just before you jump.

When you start to stick the landings consistently, you can move on to bigger jumps. Small jumps seem bigger if you spring into the air. Approach the jump compressed and pop upward as you leave the lip. This gives you some extra height and keeps your body forward and over the board. When landing, keep your weight centered and land with the tail down first to cushion the impact of your board to the snow. (The tail of the snowboard absorbs shock much the same way as the leaf spring on your car. It takes the shock and spreads it out over the entire length of the snowboard.) After the tail absorbs the initial impact of the landing, inertia will gradually lay the board's center and tip sections onto the snow.

Bigger airs take more time and more practice. The bigger the air the more dangerous it can be. Move upward one step at a time, and listen to your body. It will tell you what you can or can't do.

Trees

Try walking on a two-by-four lying on the ground. No big deal, huh? Now, suspend that two-by-four twenty feet up in the air and try walking on it. Your eyes stare at the ground and the fear factor sets in. The same thing goes for trees. Out on the groomed slopes you can turn wherever and whenever you want. But if you toss in a thin grove of trees, your eyes draw you to them like a magnet and your body follows.

For the advanced snowboarder, trees harbor a freeriding playground. You can veer off into the trees to find the last of the deep, ungroomed powder while the crowds are flattening the snow on the groomed trails. If you like to turn, a grove of trees is the place to do it. Trees are nature's slalom gates, forcing you to turn and to keep turning.

The key to snowboarding in the trees is to concentrate on the fall line, not on the trees. Set up a

Charles Arnell finds a clean route through the trees.
JOHN KELLY

CLIFFS

Cliff jumps look spontaneous in videos and movies. That's because all you usually see is the edited version of the film. You rarely get to see all of the scouting and the planning—or the terrifying crashes. Jumping off cliffs involves a certain amount of danger, so you have to be able to calculate the risks and judge your own capabilities.

Don't just go out and start jumping off cliffs. Start small and work your way up. When you find a cliff, check out the approach and the landing. If they look OK, get your gear and body ready. Check your bindings and board, and make sure everything is tight. Next, stretch out your body, warm up your knees, and get psyched. Since jumping is just as much mental as it is physical, if you think you're going to fall, you will. So, imagine a perfect jump and landing.

In the air, stay compressed, spot your landing, and get ready to absorb the hit. Reach for the landing with your legs and absorb the impact with your knees. If you lose control, try sitting back to save yourself. Do a butt check or bounce your butt off the tail of the board. Check your speed if you have to, and save enough adrenaline for the next big jump.

—Matt Goodwill, 1993 World Extreme Snowboarding Champion

NIGHT SNOWBOARDING

Some ski areas can turn night into day by focusing hundreds of giant spotlights on their trails. Snowboarding at night can be a real gas. Lift tickets cost less, the crowds are thinner, and the lift lines are shorter. The tradeoff for the extra time on the slopes can be lower visibility and icier conditions.

When snowboarding at night, leave your tinted goggles at home and use clear goggles or sport shields. When you're on the slopes, mellow out a bit. It may be tougher to see that next bump, gully, or even fellow snowboarders. Other than that, the mountain is yours. Enjoy!

—*Scott Downey*

short, fast rhythm in your turns and bounce from one turn to the next. When the snow is deep and powdery, use each bounce to get your board to the surface, and turn on top of the snow. If the snow is packed down, make tight turns in the open gullies between trees. Keep your speed down, and use check turns to stay in control.

The fall line is your friend in the trees. Long traverses sap your energy and cause hesitation—big drawbacks in the trees. So if you find yourself heading for a tree, you'll often be better off taking the fall line route around it than traversing up and around it. Still, let the terrain, the obstacles, and your own instincts tell you where to go.

6 Out of Bounds

Backcountry Snowboarding

Blowin' some "smoke" high in the New Zealand Alps. PHOTO OF CHRIS GALLARDA BY JOHN KELLY

Not so very long ago, ski resorts didn't allow snowboarders on their slopes. The only way to go snowboarding was to find your own mountain, hike up it, and ride back down. Today, backcountry snowboarding takes you back to the roots of the sport—and at the same time, propels you to the cutting edge. That's right: far beyond the lift lines and crowded slopes, a whole new world of snowboarding beckons. And if you're hungry enough to go after it, backcountry snowboarding can push your adrenaline level to new heights.

Backcountry snowboarding is more than a trip out of bounds. It can involve mountaineering on the way up, and challenging riding on the way down. It requires avalanche awareness to avoid trouble, and group unity to help those

Josh Skolnick rides untracked terrain near Snowbird, Utah. JOHN KELLY

who do get into trouble. Backcountry riding also calls for some new skills and new tools to get you in and out safely.

Backcountry Skills

Because backcountry terrain is not neatly groomed and contoured to meet the needs of casual resort snowboarders, riding conditions can demand the most of your skills. Untrammeled backcountry snow can be softer and deeper than what you will find on resort trails. Your board may sink deeper into the fluffy white stuff than you're used to, and every turn may take a little extra time and effort. Backcountry runs are often full of trees that demand precise turning skills. You may also need to turn in narrow chutes or slice through tight passages between rocks. Finally, backcountry access often involves traversing to your desired line. Since this can involve traversing through very deep snow or across narrow ledges, your traversing and gliding skills need to be well developed.

You can practice backcountry snowboarding skills by taking short, calculated runs though the

trees at your local resort. Once you are capable of turning in deep untracked snow between the trees and around rocks, your skills may be good enough for the backcountry.

If you expect to run into deep, fresh powder in the backcountry, consider using a board that is larger than the one you normally use at the resorts. Your normal board may not float well in powder, and it may be difficult to keep the nose above the snow. Also consider offsetting your stance to the rear of the board. This will help you float the nose and sink the tail deeper into the snow no matter what length of snowboard you choose.

Backcountry Access

There are a number of principal ways to gain access to the backcountry. Let's take a look at them.

Many resorts have special trails that lead to designated backcountry routes. Such trails are often marked on ski maps and can be designated as "authorized backcountry access points." If you venture into these areas, you will often end up at a road or neighboring town, and you may need to

Untrammeled snow, steep hills, and the challenge of maneuvering through trees and rocks mean intense backcountry action. PHOTO OF J. J. COLLIER BY STEVE WANKE

walk to local access points. So be sure you know where you're going, and plan ahead of time for your return to the resort. If you're not sure where the best routes or access points are, travel into the backcountry with someone familiar with the area.

Another way to access the backcountry is to drive, snowmobile, or hike in from legal access points. Much of the land managed by the Forest Service is open to backcountry snowboarding and may be well suited to these types of access. Before you head out, plan your descent so that after your run, you don't need to hike upward just to get to your backcountry exit point. Once again, consider traveling with people familiar with the area.

A popular and reasonably affordable way to access great backcountry terrain is to go with a snow-cat tour operation. Hundreds of snow-cat operations around the world cater to skiers and snowboarders seeking the backcountry experience. Snow cats can take you to amazing fields of untracked powder and pick you up at the bottom of a run. All you do is get back in the snow cat, relax,

and enjoy the 10- to 20-minute ride back to the top of the hill. Just keep in mind that snow cats usually travel on snow-covered logging roads, so although the snow cats' range is good, you still may need to hike a little beyond the logging roads to get to the best snowboarding lines.

For the ultimate backcountry snowboarding experience, try going to the top of a mountain via helicopter. Heli-boarding is a totally awesome life experience! A helicopter can take you to just about any peak or slope that has enough landing room. It can reach areas that are inaccessible by any other means, providing some of the most exhilarating terrain you may ever encounter.

The helicopter ride itself is breathtaking, with the bird whisking you from the base of one run to the top of another in just a minute or two. Almost all helicopter operations have guides to help you make the most of your experience. They are familiar with the terrain, know where the best lines are found, and can help you steer clear of areas rife with avalanche hazards.

Larger snowboards can help riders float better when the backcountry powder gets this deep. PHOTO OF JOSH SKOLNICK BY JOHN KELLY

Backcountry Safety

Gear

In this era of high-tech equipment, it's no surprise that snowboarders have a lot of backcountry mountaineering tools available to them. These tools make climbing easier and safer. You'll also need a selection of other special equipment and supplies for your backcountry adventures.

The Basics

Out in the backcountry, you'll need some items you would never think of back on the groomed slopes of ski resorts, with their day lodges, restaurants, safety patrols, and other amenities.

Away from it all, you'll want to have a *first-aid kit, food, water,* and *extra clothing*—and a *pack* to carry it all in. A *map* of the area plus a *compass* will help you stay oriented to your location. And don't forget the *sunblock.*

Protective eyewear is essential. *Goggles* are commonly used at ski resorts, but they can be especially beneficial in the backcountry. Not only do some tinted goggles offer a measure of protection from the sun, but they also keep wind and snow out of your eyes and improve visibility. They also protect your eyes from branches as you ride in the trees.

SWALLOWTAIL SNOWBOARDS

Swallowtail snowboards are designed and built specifically for the backcountry. They hark back to the early days of snowboarding when metal edges did not exist, snowboards were not allowed on resort hills, and all boarding was done in the backcountry.

The swallowtail snowboard features a split tail that works much like the keel skeg on a boat—as an aid to steering and stability. The split tail sinks deeper into the snow than a standard tail design because of the reduced surface area behind the rear foot.

Many of the newer swallowtail designs have concave bases (indented in the middle) and deep sidecuts. A concave base helps with board control, and the deep sidecut helps initiate turns more quickly. The stance is usually offset toward the rear of the board so you don't have to lean back as much as you would with a more traditional board.

All these features combine to make the swallowtail board well suited to backcountry powder riding. However, the board does not work well on any surface other than moderate to deep powder. If the terrain or conditions are not right for a swallowtail, stay with a conventional board.

—*Charles Arnell*

Snowboarders trek toward their waiting helicopter. Helicopters provide fast, easy access to otherwise inaccessible backcountry terrain. PHOTO OF CHARLES ARNELL AND JOSH HEMINGER BY JOHN KELLY

Helmets are a great idea in the backcountry. They can, and do, save lives during unexpected collisions with rocks, trees, or other obstacles.

Optional Equipment

Depending on conditions, any number of mountaineering and safety tools might be invaluable in the backcountry.

If access to your snowboarding area means wading through soft snow, consider using *snowshoes*. If you expect ice, you can bring *crampons*. *Collapsible trekking poles* or an *ice ax* can help with balance over rough terrain and safety on slippery slopes. *Avalanche transceivers*, and training in how to use them, can be lifesavers in an emergency. And *shovels* could be needed to free a buddy trapped in the snow.

Training

Before you take a snowboarding trip into the backcountry, educate yourself about mountain safety.

Dan Ray works for his line in the Alaska backcountry. Mountaineering skills and physical conditioning make it easier to climb backcountry terrain. JOHN KELLY

FIRST DESCENTS

Many *first descents*—the first time a particular run is completed—involve conditions that scared previous snowboarders away: steep slopes, narrow chutes, unstable snow, and difficult lines. So maximizing your chance of success may depend on minimizing the risks involved. Plan the entire descent route before you attempt it. You should be able to visualize the entire run before you actually commit to the descent. When you start your descent, maintain an even speed so that you don't fatigue early or fall.

Avalanches can be the most serious hazard you'll face. Since avalanches follow the fall line, stay to the sides of chutes and couloirs. If you see a fracture or slide begin, ride toward high rocks and ridges for safety.

The *danger time* during a first descent is *any* time you're in there riding. In other words, a two-minute descent has 33 percent less danger time than a three-minute descent.

Know your limits, and don't be afraid to push them. Sometimes the greatest efforts bear the greatest rewards.

—*Scott Downey*

Craig Kelly and Matt Goodwill enjoy the backcountry at Iddings Park in Montana's Crazy Mountains. Lonnie Ball, courtesy Montana Powder Guides

You'll find a good number of books on backcountry travel. Mountaineering schools offer courses on alpine ascents, glacier travel, and avalanche avoidance (and rescue). These courses teach techniques of backcountry travel that can help you understand and respect the mountain environment and make your travels safer. If courses aren't available in your area, hook up with people who can oversee your safety.

Group Travel

Since nobody's looking over your shoulder in the backcountry, you've got to watch out for your own safety. Take all your basic safety procedures to the max.

Let others know where you're going and when you'll return. Travel in groups of two, three, or more people and stay within visual contact. It's a good idea to have handheld radios for your group so that each member can communicate with the others. Make sure you can hear and see each other whether you're in trees, deep powder, or open bowls. The only time you should make a point of keeping a large separation between party members is in potentially dangerous sections—such as slopes prone to avalanches. That way, the

Dan Ray airing it out in the backcountry. JOHN KELLY

Charles Arnell finds a line between a rock and a soft spot.
JOHN BING

rest of the group can offer help if one person gets in trouble.

Avalanches

You need to answer a simple question before you descend any slope capable of producing an avalanche: *Is it safe?*

The answer lies in terrain analysis, snow stability evaluation, avalanche weather forecasting, and route selection. Sometimes the answer is easy: a narrow, steep gully topped by a fresh, heavily loaded cornice represents an avalanche waiting to happen. Other times, a slope hides the answer beneath innocent-looking layers of snow or a moderate incline.

The only way to understand avalanches is to educate yourself. If you ride with mountain guides, follow their instructions, and try to learn from them. If you plan to go into the backcountry without a seasoned guide, first take a course on avalanche safety, study books on the subject, and inspect local avalanche conditions with people who can reveal the snow's secrets.

One final point: despite all the knowledge you may acquire about avalanche safety, avalanches will always remain a calculated risk.

7 Satisfying That Urge
Freestyle

A contorted backside air. DENNIS CURRAN/SPORTS FILE

Look how far you've come! Your snowboard feels like an extension of your body, and you're carving the slopes with ease. Freeriding is a blast whether you're floating big turns through fresh powder or darting in and out of moguls. But you've seen some riders pull off skateboard-style tricks on the snow, others bonking and grinding logs, rails, and boxes in the snowboard park. Now that's what *you* want to do. What you've got is the jib-bonk urge!

Welcome to the world of freestyle—a world where spinning, sliding, bonking, and grinding are the norm. A world where skateboard-influenced tricks rule the slopes, and where new tricks are born every day. In this chapter we're going to learn all the standard freestyle tricks, and lay down the foundation for more advanced tricks. You can take this stuff with you into the halfpipe chapter or spend the rest of your days searching for that perfect trick. No matter what you do, this

Noah Salasnek does a shifty at Mount Rose, Nevada.
TREVOR GRAVES

chapter will add to your snowboarding repertoire and blast open a new realm of riding opportunities.

Some Important Terminology

Freestyle tricks have a language unto themselves. To understand the tricks, you've got to learn lingo like *frontside*, *backside*, and *blindside*.

If you're *spinning frontside*, you're turning the same way you would for a heelside turn (counterclockwise for regulars, clockwise for goofies). *Spinning backside* or *blindside* means you're turning the same way you would for a toeside turn (clockwise for regulars and counterclockwise for goofies).

Picture frontside and blindside spins in your head before moving on. This will make many of the tricks in this chapter easier to comprehend.

Edge Awareness

The most important part of freestyle riding is edge awareness. Edge awareness lets you spin, turn, and

land airs when you want to, not just when you're feeling lucky. Your edges are your friends when you're carving clean turns, but they're your enemies when you hook them in the snow.

Before you can start doing freestyle tricks, you've got to know how to turn and know where your edges are at all times. Spinning and riding fakie are two great ways to improve your feel for your edges. We're going to proceed step-by-step through progressively harder spin tricks and fakie exercises until you can finally mix and match advanced freestyle tricks on your own.

Ground Spins

You've probably spun quite a few times already—whether intentionally or by accident—so spins will

SPINNING

If someone tells you, "Spinning is all in your head," they're right. As long as you're looking over your shoulder in the direction you're spinning, your body will continue to spin. To stop your rotation, you have to stop your head and look in the direction you want to go.

—*Scott Downey*

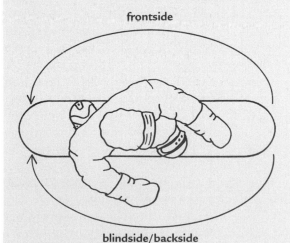

There are two ways to spin your body: frontside *and* blindside *(or* backside*).*

be easy to learn. Still, we're going to start slow and easy, and take our first 360-degree spin one step at a time.

Start a 360 with a toeside or heelside turn but keep turning the board all the way uphill. When your board stalls out, you'll have a chance to get your bearings. From there, flatten your board, look in the direction of your spin, and push your front foot in that direction. Your board will spin another 180 degrees and finish up the revolution.

Pick a short run and practice linking 360s all the way down the hill. Go slowly at first, and increase your speed gradually. Once you're comfortable spinning one way, try spinning in the opposite direction.

Riding Fakie (Switch Stance)

The next step toward total edge control involves some more practice riding *fakie* or *switch stance* (they mean the same thing). Being able to ride fakie will bail you out of a lot of problems—like when you only make it halfway through a 360-degree spin. Plus it will open up the door to a lot of tricks that start or end fakie.

Riding fakie basically involves putting your back leg in front of you and riding as if it were your front leg. If you're regular, you'll be riding like you were goofy, and vice versa (that's why they call it switch stance). The problem is that everything will feel weird again—as if you were learning to snowboard from scratch. That's OK. We've got a couple of drills that will help you improve quickly.

Back in chapter 4, you practiced traversing both forward and fakie. Go back and try that drill again. If you want to traverse fakie, put more weight on your back foot, put your hands over the tail, and look where you want to go. That will be enough to start traversing fakie.

If you make each fakie traverse steeper than the last, you'll soon want to add garland turns to check your speed. Make these turns the same way you did your first skidded turns: shift your weight forward (*forward* now means *toward the tail* of the board), look in the direction of the turn, and steer with your feet. The more you practice, the more comfortable your turns will feel. Before you start linking your

turns, however, check out this next exercise (and take a look at the accompanying photos of the snowboarder turning into a fakie traverse).

Start by traversing on your toe edge. Begin a heelside turn, but push your back leg all the way around the outside of the turn until it ends up in front. Now you're riding fakie on your toe edge, and you're heading in the opposite direction. To get back to your toe edge riding forward, begin a switch-stance heelside turn, spin your *new* back leg around 270 degrees (three-quarters of a circle), and you'll be doing another forward toeside traverse. If you're doing the drill correctly, you'll traverse on the same edge (the heel edge or the toe edge) in both directions.

You can do this drill any way you want to—starting heelside first, or toeside first; starting fakie first, or forward first. When it feels comfortable, you will be ready to link turns riding fakie down the fall line. Soon you'll be able to mix 360s and fakie turns in any combination you want.

Wheelies and Slides

Wheelies

Tail wheelies lay down a foundation for a lot of tricks. To do a tail wheelie, lean way back on your board and pull the tip up off the snow. Just like on

Tail wheelies *lay down the foundation for many freestyle tricks.*

*Riding **fakie** (switch stance) is fun, and it opens the door to many freestyle tricks. This goofy-foot snowboarder is turning from a forward traverse into a fakie traverse. He starts his turn from a forward toeside traverse (1), then begins a heelside turn (2). He pushes his back leg all the way around the outside of the turn (3, 4, and 5) in order to bring the back leg up in front (6). The boarder is now heading in the opposite direction (7), still on his toe edge but now traversing fakie.*

a bike, the better you get, the longer you'll be able to hold it up. Once you have your tail wheelies mastered, you can turn around and do switch-stance tail wheelies on your tip.

Blunt Nose Slides

Once you're comfortable doing wheelies, you can turn them sideways and slide snow berms, small ridges, or the edge of cat tracks balanced over your tip. These sideways tip wheelies are called blunt nose slides.

Start this trick by sliding your board sideways (90 degrees to your direction of travel) while keeping your body facing downhill. Next, get low to the board, put your weight on your front leg, and pull your back foot up. If you've done it right, you'll be sliding on the front third of your board with your tail in the air. Keep your arms out for balance and hang in the sideways wheelie position as long as you can. Finish the trick by spinning back to normal—or create your own variations.

There are four main variations of the blunt nose slide. You can slide blunt on your nose (blunt nose slide) or on your tail (switch-stance blunt nose slide). You can also slide blunt on your nose or tail with your back going downhill.

*To do a **blunt nose slide**, slide your board sideways, put your weight on your front leg, and pull your back leg up. You'll end up sliding on the front third of your board with the tail in the air.*

*A snowboarder can kick up a rooster tail of snow while doing a **layback slide**.*

Layback Slides and Slashes

Layback slides have been around for a long time in both surfing and skateboarding circles. Snowboarders have added their trademark to the trick by kicking up snowy rooster tails whenever they pull off a strong layback.

A small frontside wall or embankment provides a great place to attempt your first layback. Approach the wall on your uphill edge. When you're ready, lean back toward your tail and kick your back foot forward (downhill). Support yourself with your back hand down against the snow until you can pull your board back under your body. If you're doing it right, you'll be kicking snow off the wall with the board's edge.

If you do the same trick with your back facing downhill, it is called a *backside slash*.

Getting off the Snow and into the Air

Ollies

An ollie is a basic (but very important) way of getting airborne. It's like jumping, but it uses the tail of the snowboard for some extra spring. Here's how it works:

Start cruising along in a straight line. Before you ollie, compress into a slight crouch. Jump up, bringing your front foot up first and driving it forward through the air. (Lifting your front foot first loads up energy in the tail and provides some spring for your jump.) Level out the board in the air by bringing both knees to your chest. Finish your ollie by landing with both feet on the ground at the same time.

Practice ollies every day. They'll launch you over small rocks, stumps, and other obstacles that you couldn't normally jump. They'll also teach you some of the moves used in more advanced freestyle and halfpipe tricks.

Nollies (Nose Ollies 180)

A nollie is basically just an ollie off your nose (tip). It can be combined with a 180-degree spin so that you can end the trick riding fakie.

Start a nollie by shifting your weight forward, straightening your front leg, and pulling your back leg up to ollie off your nose. You can add a 180-degree spin (frontside or backside) to finish the trick riding fakie.

Nose and Tail Rolls

Nose and tail rolls are sliding 180 spins off either end of your board. For a nose roll, shift your weight over your front leg, straighten your front leg, and

OLLIES

Ollies show up everywhere in freestyle tricks. They launch you onto rails, over rocks, and into aerial tricks. Strong ollies start with a powerful spring off your back foot, followed by a leveling of the board by bringing both knees to your chest. They end with a quiet landing on both feet. Once you can ollie, you can add spins or grabs and begin to learn a whole slew of freestyle tricks.

—Mike Estes,
*1991 Japan Open Halfpipe Champion
and 1989 All Japan Mogul Champion*

pull your back leg up. At the same time, slide your board 180 degrees frontside or backside to end riding fakie.

A tail roll is essentially a switch-stance nose roll. It starts fakie and ends forward.

Airs with Spins

Air to Fakie

An Air to Fakie is the air version of the nollie—a 180 Air that starts riding forward and ends up riding fakie. This is a simple maneuver to learn without having to get much air. To pull off your first Air to

An **ollie** is a basic, but very important, way of getting airborne. Start in a slight crouch. Next, jump up with your front foot first and drive it forward through the air. That loads up energy in the tail and gives you some spring. Level the board out in the air by bringing your knees to your chest. Finish by landing on both feet.

*A **nose roll** is a 180-degree spin sliding on the nose of the board.*

Fakie, ride across the fall line on your uphill edge, jump, and throw your back foot around in front of you. Keep looking in the same direction throughout the trick to keep your balance while your body makes the spin.

Caballerials

A Caballerial is a halfpipe trick named after pro skateboarder Steve Caballero. The freestyle and freeriding version of a Caballerial is a 180 Air that starts fakie and ends riding forward (like a tail roll, but with more air). Many snowboarders call this trick a *half-Cab* because the halfpipe version of a Caballerial—discussed in chapter 8—is a 360 Air.

360 Airs

If you've got it all together, you can try your first complete spin in the air. In the 360 Air—also known as a *360* or a *Helicopter*—you wind up your body and start the spin just as you leave the jump. Keep your

*A **Caballerial** is a halfpipe trick named after pro skateboarder Steve Caballero. The freestyle or freeriding version of the trick—shown above—is a 180 Air that starts fakie and ends forward.*

upper body low and look in the direction of the spin until you spot the landing. When you complete the spin, touch down softly and ride away!

If you've mastered riding fakie, you can do a *Fakie to Fakie 360* by starting and ending riding fakie.

540 Airs

Now you're getting into the big leagues. The 540 Air is a spin-and-a-half that usually starts out forward and ends up fakie. However, you can do 540s starting fakie and end up riding forward. Once you master the 540, you can keep adding rotations. Top riders throw 720s (two full spins) regularly, and some riders can even spin 900 degrees (two and a half spins) and stick the landing!

Mix It Up

Shifties

In skateboarding, a shifty is a trick that spins the board 180 degrees under the rider's feet without switching the stance. Snowboarding's version of a shifty is a little bit different. Here's how it works.

Once you're in the air, twist your upper and lower body in opposite directions. (Your upper body will look like it's riding fakie, while your lower body will look like it's riding normal.) Hang in the air like that, then spin the board back under your upper body at the last possible second to land. The whole coil/recoil motion makes up the shifty.

You can add shifties to tricks like blunt nose slides and wheelies to come up with new trick combinations.

Reverts and Late Spins

Reverts and late spins fit into the same category as shifties—but reverts are done on the snow (following a jump), while late spins are done in the air.

Shifties lay the groundwork for late spins by teaching you how to coil and recoil your body in the air. In a basic late 180, you hold back on your last half-spin until you're

SPINNING IN THE AIR

Keep two things in mind whenever you're spinning in the air. First, approach each jump low and compact, and don't stand too tall as you leave the lip. If you do, you may swim through the air and fall sideways. Second, use your arms to help you spin faster or slower. Spread your arms out just before you jump, then spin them in the direction you want your body to spin as you leave the lip. The closer to your body you hold your arms in the air, the faster you'll spin.

—*Scott Downey*

just about to land, then powerfully spin the board around to stick the landing.

A basic revert is a late 180 spin on the snow that takes you from riding fakie back to riding normal, or vice versa. Since you're landing a jump before you revert, it's easy to land too flat, jam an edge in the snow, and fall. You'll have a wider margin for error if you land in a wheelie position and spring your board before you revert, or revert on a bump.

To do a **shifty**, twist your upper and lower body in opposite directions. PHOTO OF JEFF BRUSHIE BY JON FOSTER

Airs with Grabs

Now you're really starting to get the hang of jumping, and you're eager to move onto bigger tricks. One great way to get ready for grabs is to practice long and hard on a trampoline. See the sidebar on page 96 for the particulars.

Sidekicks and Tucks

The first step in moving into tougher tricks is to *pop* harder off the ground when you ollie or jump. This adds height and hang time to your airs, and gives you a chance to think about new tricks like sidekicks and tucks.

To do a sidekick, try to kick yourself in the butt with your board during a jump. For a tuck, pull your knees toward your chest mid-jump. Both tricks lay the foundation for many halfpipe tricks by teaching you to bring the board up to your hand for grabs, so make sure they become second nature.

Boning and Pokes

Whenever you straighten out one or both legs, it's called boning. If you straighten your front leg, it's called a *nose bone* or *nose poke*. If you straighten out your back leg it's called a *tail bone* or *tail poke*.

You've already learned how to bone a few of your tricks—like the blunt nose slides and tail

*Shawn Snoke does a **nose bone**—or nose poke—by boning (straightening) his front leg.* JAMES CASSIMUS

BONING

Boning or poking out your snowboard is easy: it's all in the hips. If you want to do a simple nose bone, grab your board with your rear hand between your feet on your toeside edge. As you reach to make the grab, rotate your front hip away from the toe edge, across the width of the board, and your front leg will automatically stretch out and stiffen. Rotating a hip to bone out your airs makes grabbing easy, helps you to maintain balance, and lets you land your airs clean.

—*Charles Arnell*

Chris Noyes makes a big tail grab in the skies over Mount Hood. JEFF CURTES

wheelies (you straightened one leg in both of those tricks). You can now add some style to tricks like shifties and half-Cabs by boning one of your legs. When you get to the halfpipe chapter, you'll find that boning makes some tricks easier to grab.

Grabs

Once you get your sidekicks, tucks, and bones down, you can begin to grab your board just like you practiced on the trampoline. Grabs are just like they sound: you reach down and grab your board with your hand while you're in the air.

The better you are at bringing your board to your body, the easier it is to grab your board. That's because it's already close to your hand.

Don't worry where or how you grab your board for now; do whatever feels good when you are airborne. Once you can do a few grabs and land without falling, you can flip ahead to the tricks described in chapter 8 or in the Appendix. Many halfpipe grabs work equally well when you're out freeriding. Freeriding and freestyle versions of halfpipe tricks often have the same names, so your friends will be able to tell your *Mutes* from your *Methods* when your hands meet your board.

Riding Obstacles Other than Snow

In the not too distant past, snowboarders looked at objects like logs and handrails as board-wreckers— gnarly obstacles just waiting to steal a chunk of your P-Tex base. Nowadays, snowboarders ollie up onto rails, slider bars, boxes—anything *legal and nondestructive*—then slide, spin, and dismount. Once you try it, you'll understand why they're having so much fun.

The perfect place to ride obstacles is at a *snowboard park*. Snowboard parks have it all: slider bars, boxes—even trash cans and logs. You can hit everything, and it's legal. Don't go around sliding the handrail at the lodge or grinding the bark off all the trees. You'll get your lift ticket pulled and give your fellow snowboarders a bad name.

With a toeside grab, a boarder takes to the air. GREG SCHMITT

Rail Slides

There are countless ways to slide or grind slider bars, rails, and logs. That's the great thing about them. You can even combine tricks like spins or wheelies with your grinds to come up with new trick combinations. Still, there are six basic grinds that provide the basis for more advanced tricks. Here they are:

1. *50/50*: The snowboard rides parallel with the rail, traveling straight down it. Skateboarders dubbed this trick the 50/50 to describe grinding both skateboard axles at the same time. The 50/50 is the safest way to learn rail slides since the chances are minimal that you'll catch an edge.

2. *Five-O Grind*: A wheelie on the rail in the 50/50 position.

3. *Rock-n-Roll Grind*: The snowboard is straight across the rail, and the rail is halfway between your feet. Since your edges are grinding the rail, keep the front edge up. Otherwise it will catch the rail and you'll slam.

4. *Smith Grind*: Like a rock-n-roll, but the tip is lower and more forward than the tail.

TRAMPOLINE TRAINING

Before you take flight on your snowboard, learn air awareness in a controlled environment—like on a nice, bouncy trampoline.

The trampoline is the secret weapon of the freestyle elite. Almost all of the world's top freestylers practiced their moves on trampolines. Many of them perfected their basic grabs, learned new grabs, and learned to tweak and bone their grabs on trampolines. Whenever you want to learn a new move, learning it on the trampoline first will let you stick it on the snow much faster.

Before you climb aboard a trampoline with a snowboard, put a protective layer of tape around the board's edges so you don't tear up the mat. Wear your normal snowboard boots so you can develop a real feel for your tweaks and grabs.

Start every session by just bouncing straight up and down to get a feel for landing on the trampoline with a snowboard attached to your feet. Once you're warmed up, practice spinning around on every other bounce. If you can't spin all the way around, just spin halfway. Keep your body upright and your board below you at all times. Turn your head in the direction you're spinning each time, and let your body follow your head through the spin.

After you feel well balanced on the trampoline, you can practice basic grabs. Jump up and bring the board toward your chest by bending your knees. Keep your back straight and avoid looking down at your feet; looking down may make you lose balance. Once you're comfortable with bringing the board up toward your body, drop your rear hand down and grab an edge between your front and rear foot. Though you may be able to grab an edge for only a split second during your initial attempts, you will quickly learn to hang onto it longer the more you practice.

As you become more comfortable, strive to easily grab your board on the way up and give a good tug with your hand without letting go of the edge. As you start to come back down, let go with your hand and drop your legs to meet with the mat on impact.

Eventually try to alternate between grabbing the board with your front and rear hands. And try grabbing the snowboard in different places. Grab the tail with your rear hand, then the tip with your front hand. Try every conceivable grab you can imagine, and feel free to invent your own.

As you progress into more advanced grab moves, keep in mind that bending your knees brings the board up to your hands—and that leaning over or reaching out for the board will only throw you off balance.

—*Charles Arnell*

There are many ways to grind slider rails, bars, and logs. Here, Dave Collier does a Smith grind. COURTESY MOUNT HOOD SNOWBOARD CAMP

Shawn Snoke does a rock-n-roll grind down a log. James Cassimus, courtesy Sims Snowboards

There are limitless variations of freestyle tricks. Take an old trick, bone a leg, grab it a new way, and let your imagination flow. Photo of Dave Collier courtesy Mount Hood Snowboard Camp

5. *Nose Slide*: Like a rock-n-roll, but the rail is between your front foot and the nose.

6. *Tail Slide*: Like a rock-n-roll, but the rail is between your back foot and the tail.

Bonking

Still searching for some extra style? Something to make the next rider say, "Wait! What was that?!" Bonk! When you're passing over a box or getting ready to dismount a rail, slap it with your board. Push your leg down to hit the object, then lift off again so the rest of your board doesn't touch. If you hit with your nose, it's a *nose bonk*. Slap it with your tail, and it's a *tail bonk*.

8 Vertical Tricks

Riding the Halfpipe

Gian Simmen in the Men's Snowboarding Halfpipe competition at the Nagano Winter Olympic Games. JAMIE SQUIRE/ ALLSPORT

I f you're serious about catching air, going vertical, and doing tricks, there's nothing that compares to halfpipes. These long U-shaped bowls rocket riders toward the sky with sloped transitions and vertical walls. Drop in, ride up a wall, and launch!

Snowboarding halfpipes are deeply rooted in skateboarding halfpipes. In fact, if you skateboard, this chapter will feel familiar. You'll recognize parts of the halfpipe and a lot of the halfpipe tricks. But in the past, snowboard halfpipes were little more than snaky, poorly formed ravines. Before 1987, halfpipes were built above the ground with two sloped ridges of snow forming the outside walls. All that changed at the 1987 Breckenridge World Cup when Scott Downey introduced the first in-the-ground halfpipe with big, vertical walls and roll-out-style skateboard decks.

Today's halfpipes are better than ever. Special machines like the "pipe dragon" are used by many resorts to carve out perfectly shaped halfpipes, while specialized handheld tools are used to put on the finishing touches. Olympic standards and specifications now ensure consistency in halfpipes for professional competitions. Innovation and standardization mean better halfpipes, both at the competition and resort levels.

An Introduction to the Halfpipe

At first glance, halfpipes are nothing more than long, tilted, U-shaped snow trenches. But as you can see in the diagram at right, each part of the pipe has a specific name. By learning the parts of a pipe first, you'll be able to follow the lessons in this chapter. And the next time you ask another rider how to execute a trick, you'll be able to understand the explanation.

Terje Haakonsen performs a frontside air. ROB GRACIE

Snowboarding has been heavily influenced by the sports of skateboarding and surfing. Note the similarity between the skateboard and snowboard tricks shown here. PHOTO (LEFT) OF SKATER FRANK WELLS BY CRAIG CAMERON OLSEN; PHOTO (RIGHT) OF J. J. COLLIER BY JOHN KELLY

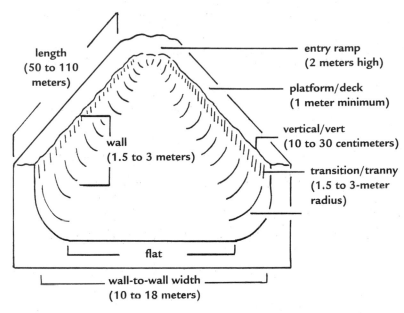

length
(50 to 110
meters)

entry ramp
(2 meters high)

platform/deck
(1 meter minimum)

vertical/vert
(10 to 30 centimeters)

wall
(1.5 to 3 meters)

transition/tranny
(1.5 to 3-meter
radius)

flat

wall-to-wall width
(10 to 18 meters)

A regulation-size halfpipe.

There are three basic sections of a halfpipe: the *flat*, the *transitions*, and the *walls*.

The flat is the center floor of the pipe. Riders spend a good chunk of time there riding from wall to wall or brushing off snow after their last fall.

The transitions—or *trannies*—are the curved sections between the flat and the vertical walls. Think of them as ramps that take you from the flat up onto the walls.

The walls are the vertical sections of the halfpipe. The steepest section of the wall is called the *vertical—vert* for short—and the top of the wall is known as the *lip*.

In addition to the flat, trannies, and walls, most halfpipes have a *deck*, or *platform*. The deck is the flat ground just past the lip of the wall. It provides an area for bailing out if you jump too far over the lip, and also serves as a great place for spectators to hang out and watch hot riders strut their stuff.

Building a Halfpipe

In times past, you were lucky if a ski resort provided an area for snowboarders to build a halfpipe. Today, the halfpipe machines used by many resorts cut out perfectly shaped halfpipes in a few hours.

Halfpipes that are going to be used in sanctioned halfpipe competitions are built to standardized size specifications. Standardization helps snowboarders fine-tune their tricks by providing some uniformity from one halfpipe to the next. Take a look at the halfpipe illustration and specifications to get a feel for the size of an average halfpipe.

Halfpipe Etiquette

Though you probably won't have to worry about collisions with the carving crowd, you've still got to play by the rules to be safe around halfpipes. Sometimes this simply means treating the halfpipe with respect, other times it means watching out for other snowboarders.

A well-maintained halfpipe is a joy to ride, while rutted walls and deep footprints screw up the fun for everyone. Never cut ledges or steps in the walls. If you fall during a run, move out of the way before the next rider enters the pipe. Don't climb

Building the first halfpipe for the summer season on Oregon's Mount Hood. Courtesy High Cascade Snowboard Camp

HALFPIPE BASICS

The most important step in learning to ride the halfpipe begins out on the slopes. Learn to use both edges in your turns and practice your 180s and 360s on the slopes. After that, the best way to start riding halfpipes is to go to a camp that teaches you how to properly ride them. Camps use drills to build up your frontside and backside skills evenly so that your skill level stays the same on both walls. Camp instructors can teach you basic grabs along with their many variations. From there, you can go as far as you want.

—Jimi Scott, IFS World Pro Tour
Halfpipe Champion 1992–1993

up over the edges of the wall; finish your run—even if you just ride down the middle of the halfpipe. If it's late in the day and the pipe's about to close down for the night, sideslip the transitions so they'll set up nicely by the next morning.

Most halfpipe etiquette is common sense: don't trash the pipe and don't crash into riders. That way, both you and the pipe will stay in great shape.

Your First Trip into the Halfpipe

Your first ride in a halfpipe can pump your body full of a thousand sensations, ranging from unbridled exhilaration to leg-stiffening paranoia. Don't let those glossy magazine photos of professional boarders blasting big airs fool you. Riding a halfpipe is new and different than carving turns or jumping over bumps. Take it easy. Go one step at a time and increase your comfort level gradually. Yeah, you could probably drop into a halfpipe and nail a couple of tricks right off if you're lucky. But you could also get hurt. That's why we're going to start with some basic progressions, get down all the fundamentals, *then* learn to ride like the pros!

Traverses

Using three simple steps, we'll get acquainted with halfpipe riding: *traverses* (or tic-tocs), *slide turns*, and *bunny hops*. To start your first traverse, sideslip into the top of the pipe, pause, and take a deep breath. When you're ready, look where you want to go and start a gentle forward traverse. Ride a foot or two up the first transition, then turn your head and traverse fakie to the other wall. Keep riding back and forth—forward up one wall, and fakie up the other. You don't have to ride fast, just stay in control and increase your height up each wall gradually.

After a few rides down the pipe, fine-tune your traverses by traversing the flat on your uphill edge and flattening your board as you ride up the walls. Absorb the transitions by flexing your knees, and keep looking where you want to go. These basic techniques will carry over into more advanced halfpipe tricks, so practice a lot. The more comfortable you become with the basics now, the easier it will be to advance later.

Slide Turns

One of the most important steps in learning to ride a halfpipe is learning to *roll your edges*: to approach each wall on one edge and leave the wall on the opposite edge. Slide turns teach you to roll your edges without having to jump or catch any air.

Slide turns are easier to learn (and more effective) in a halfpipe without any vertical. Look for an old pipe and start off again by sideslipping into the pipe and traversing forward toward one of the walls. Ride on your uphill edge as you traverse across the flat, then flatten your board as you ride up the transition. (If someone were standing at the bottom end of the pipe watching you, they would only see the bottom of your snowboard as you tilted it onto its uphill edge to traverse the flat.) As you approach the peak of your ascent up the wall, get ready to turn.

Slide turns are skidded turns done on the transitions or walls. Here's how they work: Pretend you're a surfer riding up a wave and turning back down. Start the turn by looking back into the pipe in the direction you want to go. Extend your legs to unpressure your board, then steer it around the turn with your feet. As you come back down the transition and onto the flat, start another traverse on your uphill edge.

Feel what your edges are doing in the turns. Ride the uphill edge as you traverse the flat, ride a flat base up the wall, and roll onto the opposite edge after you leave the wall. Approach on your heel edge, leave on your toe edge, approach on your toe edge, leave on your heel edge. Trace big Cs up and down the walls, going higher and higher up the trannies as you gain confidence. Ultimately, this will be the way you roll your edges whether you're doing little bunny hops or blasting big air.

Practice a lot and take it easy. Again, you're learning the basic skills you'll need before you can do more advanced tricks. When you're ready, we can learn to bunny hop.

Bunny Hops

It's building like a volcano—the urge to catch air. Well, we're almost there. Bunny hopping will give you your first taste of catching air in a halfpipe and bring you one step closer to launching into heart-pounding aerial displays.

When you were slide turning, you set your direction on the flat and did a sort of skidded turn on the trannies or walls. Now you'll start turning in the air instead of turning on the wall.

As with slide turns, look for an old halfpipe without any vertical. Start with another traverse on your uphill edge and flatten your board as you head up the first wall. As you reach the top of your ascent, add a little hop. Nothing big—just enough to get you airborne. To get your body to turn in the air, look back into the pipe and spot your landing. As your head turns into the pipe, your body will follow. When you hit the landing, absorb it with your knees, and set a new traverse to gear up for a bunny hop on the opposite wall.

Air Time

On your next ride, increase your air off both walls. Don't go big yet. Just make comfortable, controlled jumps off both lips. As you approach each transition, keep your body compressed and cen-

EDGES AND BASES

The only time you ride your edge in the halfpipe is when you're traversing the flat and starting up the transition. Your edges let you set your direction and aim toward your launch site on the far wall. You jump and land on a flat board. The rest of your time should be spent edging to create your direction.

If someone were standing at the bottom end of the halfpipe watching your ride, they should only see your base when you're coming across the flat. If you can keep that image in your mind, your halfpipe techniques will improve.

—*Scott Downey*

Basic body position for halfpipe riding. Courtesy Mt. Hood Meadows

You don't have to ride all the way up the walls when you first learn to ride half-pipes. Just ride up the transition, add a little bunny hop for some air, and learn what it feels like to ride the pipe before moving onto bigger airs.

centrate on the lip as you reach the top of your first air. Try to land gently on the top of the vertical with your board pointed down into the transition. This will give you the speed you need to hit the far wall.

Again, remember to roll from edge to edge each time you jump. Traverse the flat on your up-hill edge, flatten your board as you ride up the tranny, jump, land, and ride away on your new up-hill edge. If you enter the tranny on your toe edge, leave the tranny on your heel edge. This will make halfpipe riding a lot more fun and cut down on the number of profanities that cross your lips every time your face meets the flat. By the way, this basic jump is also called a *180 Air*.

tered over the board. Focus on the lip, lifting your front foot slightly as it coasts into the air and leaving from your back foot. If the walls are vertical, let your body flow up the wall, and extend upward as you reach the lip. If the walls are rounded and less vertical, you'll have to jump harder in order to avoid blowing out of the pipe and landing on the deck. (The more vert, the less you have to spring. The less vert, the more you have to spring.) Con-

Concentrate on the lip of the halfpipe while airborne in order to spot your landing area. G. BRADLEY, 9 BALL PRODUCTIONS

tricks by order of difficulty. We do start each section with easy tricks and end with very difficult tricks, but there are huge gray areas in between. If you want to get good—and avoid injuries—perfect the easy tricks before moving on to harder tricks. Save the most difficult tricks until after you've mastered everything else.

Finally, tricks should be an expression of your own ingenuity. You can mix and match them as you please, stamp each one with your own riding style, or invent your own. You can connect tricks and put together your own flowing routine. This is what keeps halfpipe riding fresh year in and year out!

Spin Tricks

Halfpipe riding is in an endless state of evolution, with new tricks pushing aside old tricks every year. When halfpipe riding first started, grab tricks were the thing to do. Spins and grabless airs drew anything from curious stares to outright ridicule. Today, anything goes. Freestyle spins are not only popular, riders stare in awe when a hot boarder pulls off a smooth 720 or combines a Mute stiffie grab with a 540 spin.

Introduction to Halfpipe Tricks

Now that you're dialed in to halfpipe riding, you're going to find yourself spending more time in the air. In the case of halfpipes, air means *freedom*—freedom to spin, flip, or grab your board as you please; freedom to learn and perfect new tricks.

Halfpipe tricks generally fit into four categories: *spin tricks* (horizontal rotation tricks like 180s, 360s, and 540s); *airs with hand grabs* (tricks like the *Method air*, *Lien air*, or *Stale Fish*); *handplants* (inverted tricks done on the lip of the halfpipe); and *inverted aerials* (back and front flips done off the walls without any handplants).

This chapter contains a basic guide to halfpipe tricks, but it's neither a rulebook nor an encyclopedia. Rather, it's an idea guide—fuel for your imagination. Because of that, we haven't listed the

SMOOTH SAILING

In many cases, airs can have less to do with how fast you go or how high you can ollie than they do with how compressed and smooth you are. A halfpipe with some good vertical will do all the work for you, so you don't need to overcompensate. Stay compressed all the way through the tranny and up the wall. When you start jumping and grabbing your tricks, your hand will already be close to your board, making grabs easier. You should even stay compressed as you come back down the wall and through the tranny. If the halfpipe has no vertical, you'll have to spring harder off the lip to make sure you land in the pipe.

—Jimi Scott, IFS World Pro Tour
Halfpipe Champion 1992–1993

This section contains enough basic tricks to wind you up and send you off spinning. Practice these tricks until you've got them down. Soon you'll be able to add grabs from later sections and come up with your own trick combinations.

Alley Oop

You just learned how to pull off 180 Airs in the last couple of sections. An Alley Oop is like a 180 Air, except that it is counter-rotated. In other words, instead of turning your body back down into the pipe like you normally would, you spin *up* the pipe in the reverse direction. This is easiest if you hit the wall as straight on as possible.

360 Air (Air to Fakie)

The halfpipe version of a 360 Air is similar to the 360 Air you learned in chapter 7, on freestyle. However, the midair turn back into the pipe forces you to land riding fakie. If landing fakie makes you nervous, try the next trick—the Caballerial—first.

Caballerial

The halfpipe version of the Caballerial is a 360 Air that starts fakie and ends forward. Approach the wall riding fakie, and launch. Whatever foot was in the back as you approached the wall comes all the way around and ends up in front when you land.

540s

Spinning 180 degrees more than in a 360, the 540 starts and ends riding forward. When doing 540s, you must start off with your weight shifted slightly forward, and aggressively commit to the trick. Next, look over your shoulder in the direction of your spin until you spot your landing. Finally, give it your all! Anything less could prove painful.

Shifties

The halfpipe version of the shifty is the same as the freestyle shifty discussed in chapter 7. Again, jump into the air with your upper body wound up op-posite your lower body. Bone your nose for style and stay like that until the last possible second. Finally, spin the board 180 degrees back to normal just before you land.

720s, 900s, and Beyond

Unless you can spin like a top, leave these multiple spins to the pros. Spins are fun and exciting, but they are very technical and are some of the hardest tricks to land board-side down.

Grab Basics

There are countless ways to grab your board—on the toe edge or heel edge, with your leading hand or trailing hand, near the tail or near the tip. In fact, there are enough grab combinations to keep you busy for years to come.

While each grab presents a new challenge, learning the names for the grabs can present an even bigger challenge. First of all, skateboarders were performing and naming most grab tricks long before snowboarders ever came along. Now, snowboarders use both snowboarding and skateboarding names for some of the same tricks and often change the names from one region to another.

This section includes most of the basic grab tricks and gives them names. Your friends might call the same grab something different, but the grab's still the same. Once you learn the grabs, you can call them whatever you want.

Grab Progressions

Most grab tricks can be broken down into five-step progressions: bring your knees up, reach down to grab the board, let go of the board, extend your legs to reach for the landing, and absorb the landing with your knees (*knees up, grab, let go, extend, absorb*). After you land, look at the far wall to find the spot you want to hit for your next trick.

Don't forget—you can add some flair to many tricks by *boning* (straightening) your front leg, back leg, or both legs. If you bone your front leg, it's called a *nose bone*. It's called a *tail bone* when you straighten your back leg. Boning adds two steps to the basic trick progression. Once the board is in

Most grab tricks can be broken down into five steps: bring your knees up, reach down and grab the board, let go of the board, extend your legs to reach for the landing, and absorb the landing with your knees. This diagram shows a regular footer doing a Mute air.

your hands, bone your trick, then pull your knees back up again before you release your board and reach for the landing. Bone your tricks at the peak of your air for maximum style.

These progressions make grabs easier by bringing your board closer to your body. They also aid your balance by keeping your body compressed and centered. Still, if all of this seems too confusing, just remember to start grabbing your board halfway through your air so that you're grabbing at the peak, and release the board as you drop back into the halfpipe.

Grab Tricks on the Frontside Wall

Since many beginners prefer riding their toe edge into their first trick, we'll learn frontside wall tricks first (right wall for regulars, left wall for goofies).

Visualize how you're going to execute your first grab trick before you drop into the halfpipe. You'll ride your uphill edge (toe edge) toward the frontside wall, flatten the board as you ride up the transition, and ride on up the wall. As you leave

the lip you'll bring your knees to your chest and grab your snowboard. On the way down, let the board go, extend your legs, and absorb the landing with your knees. Looking where you want to go will help ensure that your board turns 180 degrees in the air before you drop back into the pipe. In other words, you'll look at the lip on your approach, then look over your shoulder to find your landing.

Once you have a mental image of the basic trick progression, go ahead and try the following frontside tricks.

Frontside Air

The basic frontside air gets you ready for many of the named tricks on the frontside wall. As you leave the lip, grab the toe edge between your toes with

	Regular	Goofy
Right Wall	Frontside Wall	Backside Wall
Left Wall	Backside Wall	Frontside Wall

The first grab trick to try on the frontside wall is the frontside air. PHOTO OF JIM MORAN COURTESY MORROW SNOWBOARDS

your back hand. You can bone either leg depending on where you grab.

Crail

Grab the toe edge near the nose with your back hand. Once you become comfortable with the basic grab, bone your back leg out for style.

Lien Air

This frontside trick was developed by skateboarder Neil Blender, and still bears his name (*Lien* is Neil spelled backward). Lien describes your body position during this trick—sitting over the nose with your back leg boned—not the grab itself. However, if you hold that body position as you grab the heel edge near your tip with your front hand, some riders call the grab a Lien air.

Slob Air

Grab the toe edge near the nose with your front hand. After your first few Slobs, center your body over the nose and bone your back leg during the grab.

Stiffies

Grab the toeside edge between your bindings with either hand. When you reach the peak of your air, bone both legs straight out as if you were doing hamstring stretches or kicking out with both feet. You should be turning in the air so that you'll be able to land it.

Stale Fish

This flashy trick takes your back arm around the back of your back leg to grab the heelside edge between the bindings. Your body sits over the nose the same as it does for the Slob. You don't need too much air to make this trick work, but get a good spring off the lip.

Melanchollie Air

Grab the heel edge between your bindings with your front hand.

Grab Tricks on the Backside Wall

Many classic tricks can be done off the backside wall (left wall for regulars, right wall for goofies). Each trick uses the same progression used on the frontside wall (knees up, grab, let go, extend, absorb). Basic backside tricks are fun to do, dynamic to watch, and they lay the foundation for more difficult tricks.

Backside Air

The backside air gets you ready for tricks on the backside wall. Jump off the backside wall and turn 180 degrees back into the pipe by looking at the spot where you want to land. When you're comfortable, grab the heel edge near the nose with your front hand.

Method Air and Palmer

The next two backside tricks most riders learn are the Method air and the Palmer. In both tricks, you grab the heel edge between your heels with your

Noah Salasnek displays the freeriding version of a Melanchollie air. (For a complete list of grab tricks, see the chart in the Appendix.) Dano Pendygrasse

front hand. (Throw your free arm up and over in front of you to counteract your body's rotation.) To turn the trick into a Method air, pull the board up behind you as high as your head. Throwing the board out to the side creates the Palmer.

Mute Air

Grab the toe edge with your front hand between your toes or near the tip. Once you've got the basic grab down, bone your back leg for style and throw your back hand skyward. (If you arch your back and pull the board up behind you almost as high as your head, the Mute becomes a *Japan air*.)

Indy Air

In the basic Indy air, your back hand grabs the toe edge between your toes.

Fresh Fish

The Fresh Fish is the backside wall version of the frontside Stale Fish. At first, grab the heel edge with your back hand between your heels. At the same time, bone out your back leg. Keep your other arm straight up in the air to counterbalance everything.

Grab Variations

Backside Variations

Basic grabs are just a starting point, a vehicle for exploration. You can now start to mix grabs and redefine your tricks. For example, you can take a standard backside trick like the Indy Air and make three new tricks. If you drop your back knee to the board, it becomes an *Indy tuck knee*. If you bone your front leg, it becomes an *Indy nose bone*. The

A big Method air. SEAN SULLIVAN, PROGRESSIVE IMAGES

hardest variation of the Indy Air is the *Indy tail bone*, a back-handed toe edge grab with your back leg boned out. You can mix Mute air with a grabless trick like the Alley Oop to pull off an *Alley Oop Mute*.

Frontside Variations

If you want to expand your repertoire of tricks on the frontside wall, try some variations of the basic Slob air. By grabbing Slob with both hands, you turn the trick into a *double-handed Slob*. Once you've got that trick mastered, you can move onto a harder double-handed slob—the *Spaghetti air*. In the Spaghetti air, your back hand reaches forward through your legs to grab the toe edge next to your front hand. At the same time, you sit over the tip of the board and bone your back leg to make the trick come together.

Through-the-Legs Grabs

Reaching through your legs to grab the opposite edge might look difficult, but it can be mastered with little more effort than some of the tricks you've already learned. Here are three tricks to practice.

The first trick—a *Roast Beef*—is a through-the-legs grab to your heel edge with your back hand. Start out like you're going to grab a Stale Fish by boning out your back leg and sitting over the tip. Then, reach through your legs to grab the heel edge.

If you do the same thing with your front leg boned, it's called a *Chicken Salad*. The Roast Beef and Chicken Salad can be done on either wall.

A good backside through-the-legs trick to practice is the *Tai Pan*. In this trick, your front hand reaches through and grabs the toe edge between your toes.

More Tricks

The list of new trick combinations could go on and on. You can add grabs to spin tricks like the Alley Oop to come up with new tricks. In the *Iguana Alley Oop*, you do a normal Alley Oop while grabbing the toe edge with your back hand near the tail. If you grab at the end of the tail, it's a *tail-grab Alley Oop*. You can even throw tail grabs in with your 360s to come up with *tail-grab 360s*.

Great attitude, great altitude. J. J. Collier goes huge.
ROB GRACIE

The Appendix has a trick chart that lists many basic grabs. Use that as your starting point, then watch other riders, perfect your basic tricks, and set your imagination free. Grabbing your board will never get boring!

Handplants, Inverts, and Aerials

You've already figured out that vertical snowboarding is the name of the game in halfpipe riding. You can use the same momentum that shot you out of the pipe to get your board over your head and your hands on the lip.

Keep in mind that you're getting into some pretty advanced tricks here. There's a big difference between having your snowboard over your head and snowboarding over your head! Make sure you're comfortable with everything else in this chapter before you try handplants and aerials. Once you've got the other tricks down, you can practice these tricks.

Two-Handed Inverts and Ho-Ho's

The easiest handplant to learn is the two-handed invert. Two-handed inverts let you use both arms to support and control your handstand.

Approach the backside wall low, compressed, and fast. As you go up the lip, let the board fly skyward as your upper body cartwheels in toward the pipe. The goal is to land your hands on the lip while you're upside down. As you drop back into the pipe, twist and rotate the board back under you while pushing off the snow with your hands. Get your body centered over the board for the landing, and get ready for the next wall.

If you stall out your two-handed handplant and hold it for a long time, the same trick becomes a Ho-Ho.

Layback Air

This one-handed handplant is done on the frontside wall. It is a great trick for beginners to learn because beginners naturally tend to put their back hand down.

Ride up the wall on your toe edge. As your front foot passes the lip, reach back and plant your back hand on the lip. Your board will sail above your head. Arch your back and let it fall back into the pipe. Push off with your back hand to get your body back over your board and ride back down the transition.

Andrecht

This one-handed handplant—named after skateboarder Dave Andrecht—is done on the backside wall. Start off like you are going to do a two-handed invert, but do your handstand on your trailing hand while grabbing the board with your leading hand. If you bone out your front leg, this becomes a *sad Andrecht*. If you bone out your back leg, it's a *Bonedrecht*. Finally, if you plant your front hand instead of your back hand and grab with your back hand, the trick is called an *Eggplant*.

Frontside Invert

A frontside invert is a one-handed handplant on the frontside wall. Go up the wall, plant your front hand, and grab your toe edge with your trailing hand. Your snowboard should arc over your head, spin 180 degrees, and drop back into the pipe. If that sounds complicated, think of this trick as a frontside air with your front hand planted on the lip.

Miller Flip

This is a one-handed 180 handplant named after Darrel Miller. Ride straight at the frontside wall and plant your front hand on the lip. As your snowboard flies over your head, grab the toe edge between your toes with your back hand. Hold the handplant as long as you can, then spin the board 180 degrees and back under you for the landing.

Elguerial

The Elguerial is a fakie to forward (or forward to fakie) 360 handplant flip named after pro skateboarder Eddie Elguera. Start the trick by riding straight at the wall fakie. When you hit the lip,

Charles Arnell demonstrates a perfect frontside invert.
JON FOSTER

drop your back hand (your front hand when you're riding fakie) on the lip and let the board fly over your head. Spin the board 360 degrees and bring it back under you for the landing.

Aerials

If you can do inverts, you might be a candidate for aerials. Aerials flip you end over end without hand-plants. There are all sorts of aerials. For example, a *Crippler* is a *J-tear air* (see the sidebar at right) without a handplant. A *McTwist* is something akin to a midair barrel roll or a front-flip-540 twist.

Don't overestimate your ability to pull off aerials. They're not only quite dangerous, they're illegal at many ski areas. Perfect your handplants first and fine-tune your air awareness. Also, try your first aerials when the halfpipe is soft so that it will soften your landings.

Advanced aerials like this one can be very dangerous, but are a great display of the skill and style of today's pros.
D. W. HOLLENBECK, COURTESY HEELSIDE

THE J-TEAR

Snowboarding tricks are invented daily—a slight variation on an old trick here, a new twist there. When something revolutionary comes along, other boarders jump up and take notice.

Mike Jacoby invented the handplant called the *J-tear* quite by accident. It's not something that the average pipe rider can pull off, but Mike chuckles when he recalls the experience:

"I was out snowboarding in the pipe and wanted to learn a handplant. Since I hadn't come from a skateboarding background, I had no clue how to start. I went up the frontside wall, instead of the backside wall, flew upside down and around, and landed back on my feet. I looked back at what I did—a 540 backflip handplant—and that was it. My friends were pretty impressed. My friend Mike Gentry called it the Jacoby tear—J-tear for short."

—*Mike Jacoby, 1991 Overall World Champion; 2nd place overall, 1992 World Cup*

Quarterpipe hits let skilled riders bust out huge tricks with maximum style. Time-lapse photography helps us understand the move. D. W. HOLLENBECK, COURTESY HEELSIDE

9 Judges and Stopwatches

Snowboarding Competitions

Shannon Dunn, Bronze Medal winner in the halfpipe snow-boarding competition, Nagano Winter Olympics. NATHAN BILOW/ALLSPORT

A lot of snow has passed beneath your board by now and you're bursting with confidence. Maybe you have watched a few races or halfpipe competitions and secretly muttered, "I can do that." Well, now's the time to prove that you can.

From regional contests to the World Cup, snowboarding competitions let you push your personal envelope while vying for top rankings against rival boarders. Competitions test your skills and let you share in the camaraderie known only to a devoted contingency of aspiring snowboarders. If you're hot—*really hot*—competitions may pave your way to snowboarding stardom!

An Introduction to Snowboarding Competitions

Long before snowboards ever appeared on ski slopes, Snurfer competitions were being held at places like Pando Ski Area in Michigan. In 1982, Paul Graves launched the modern era of competitive snowboarding when he organized the National Snowboarding Championships. Held at Vermont's Suicide Six Ski Area, the National Snowboarding Championships featured slalom and downhill events.

In 1983, snowboarders were treated to two major events: the National Snowboarding Championships (organized by Jake Burton Carpenter at Vermont's Snow Valley) and the World Snowboarding Championships (organized by Tom Sims at Soda Springs Ski Bowl near California's Lake Tahoe). The World Snowboarding Championships introduced the world's first halfpipe event, forever changing competitive snowboarding. Soon, snowboarding competitions spread throughout the United States and took off in Europe. Japan enthusiastically followed these countries' leads and is now a major snowboarding country in its own right.

Competition snowboarding has exploded in popularity since the early 1980s. Snowboarding history was forever changed in 1998 when snowboarding was introduced as a full medal sport in the Olympic Games in Nagano, Japan. Many say this "legitimized" the sport of snowboarding, and all levels of snowboard competition are undoubtedly here to stay.

There are now standardized rules and sanctioning organizations for nearly every event. Whether you're a weekend warrior, an up-and-coming amateur, or a seasoned pro, you will find a variety of competitions from which to choose. Alpine racers can compete in a variety of slalom events that mimic traditional ski races while freestyle riders can cut loose in halfpipe and slopestyle competitions. There are even obstacle course, banked slalom, BoarderCross, figure eight, and extreme competitions.

This chapter introduces each type of competition, outlines basic judging and racing criteria, and passes along a few tips to help you improve your standings. If you're a spectator, this chapter will help you understand what you're watching. If you're a competitor, this chapter will get your juices flowing and make you want to go faster and higher than ever before.

ALPINE RACING RULES OF THE INTERNATIONAL SNOWBOARD FEDERATION (USSA RULES ARE IN ITALICS)

Race	Vertical Drop in Meters	Course Width in Meters	Numbers of Gates
Super G	300 to 500	30+	8% to 11% of the vertical drop (at least 30)
Giant Slalom (GS)	150 to 300 (250 to 400)	20+ (30+)	12% to 15% of the vertical drop (at least 20)
Parallel GS	150 to 300	20+	20 to 35
Slalom	120 to 220 (120 to 200)	30+ (40+)	42 to 78 (55 to 75 for men; 45 to 65 for women)
Parallel Slalom	80 to 150	20+	20 to 35

Alpine Races

Alpine races include the *super G, giant slalom (GS), parallel GS, slalom,* and the *parallel slalom.* All of these races are timed events, with the winner's circle belonging to the fastest riders. All of the race courses wind downhill through changing terrain and around gates.

To understand the basic differences between alpine races, take a look at the course chart at left. The information on that chart comes out of the rulebook for the International Snowboard Federation, considered by many to be the sanctioning organization for snowboarding events.

Other amateur and professional organizations also sponsor snowboarding events. The groups include the International Ski Federation, the United States Ski and Snowboard Association (USSA), the Professional Snowboarders Association (PSA), the United States of America Snowboard Association (USASA), and other organizations listed in the Appendix. However, these groups frequently modify the International Snowboard Federation's course standards and race rules. Accordingly, the chart adds information from USSA's rulebook in italics to show some of the differences that can exist from event to event.

As you read through the course chart, you'll notice that the vertical drop decreases as you proceed from the super G down to the slalom. At the same time, gates are crammed closer together in the slalom course than they are in the super G and giant slalom events. This translates into straighter turns and faster speeds in super G and giant slalom races, and sharper turns and slower speeds in slalom races.

Rules

Before entering any race, get an entry form, a rulebook, and a competition guide from the organization sanctioning your race. There are many things that demand special attention as you read through these materials. Before you even enter the race, you should review basic items such as entry deadlines, entry fees, race dates, and equipment restrictions. Once you enter the race, review

items such as bib requirements, ceremony attendance rules, and meeting times. Finally, find out how many runs you are allowed, where you are in the starting order, and your scheduled starting time.

Some of the most important rules deal with course inspection. You are never allowed to take practice runs on alpine race courses, so pre-race inspections are your only way to scout the course. Course inspections are only allowed during official inspection times, so know what those times are. In the super G and giant slalom, sideslipping may be the only permitted manner of inspecting the course. (When sideslipping a course, your snowboard must be sideways as you go by a gate, but it can be forward the rest of the time.) Walk-

SLALOM RACING TIPS

Good racers begin their slalom race before they ever enter the starting gate. They walk or sideslip the entire course, scout out the fastest lines, and inspect every turn. They memorize every pole, bump, and rut, then visualize their race to prepare themselves mentally.

Since slalom competitions can be won or lost by hundredths of a second, a good start is critical. Explode out of the starting gate by launching yourself into the course. Once in the course, take the fastest available line. Keep your upper body tall and quiet while your lower body drives the board through the turns. Start each turn early so that it's nearly complete as you pass each gate. If you have to turn suddenly after a gate, you might sketch, fall, or miss the next gate.

Drive for the finish line as you leave the last gate. Some extra speed can be gained by shifting your weight toward the tail of the board, but this takes lots of practice to perfect.

—*Scott Downey*

ing may be allowed in the slalom, parallel slalom, and parallel GS. No matter which manner of course inspection is permitted, you always have to wear your race bib. If you don't, you'll be disqualified.

You should also take the time to learn when and how reruns are allowed. If you find a gate down, discover problems with the timing devices, or encounter an obstruction in the course, immediately exit the course, notify the gate judge, and ask him to report it on his check card. (Don't touch the gate yourself.) If a rerun is allowed, your rerun time will supersede your previous time.

Ultimately, it's each competitor's responsibility to know, understand, and respect the rules.

Safety and Racer Responsibility

Racing and training situations are different from typical resort situations. Racers focus on speed and execution, and expect race organizers, course setters, and gate keepers to keep the race course free from hazards. Still, racers are responsible for their own safety, as well as the safety of other racers. *USSA Racer Responsibility Code*, which is reprinted below, summarizes the most important safety items. To be truly safe, you must be flexible in applying common sense, skill, and judgment to an unpredictable set of conditions.

1. Bindings must be in good condition and properly adjusted for the conditions. Unbreakable sunglasses and goggles are essential.

2. Warm up for training and racing sessions. Stretch for at least five minutes before skiing/riding. Warm up gradually on snow, making various radius turns, before skiing at racing speed.

3. Always carefully inspect a course before running it. Follow the inspection rules for the training session or race. Do not cross or go into closed courses at competitions, and always be certain that practice courses are clear before proceeding.

4. If you fall and are unhurt, immediately signal that you are OK and quickly move a safe distance away from the course. Collect your gear and reorganize away from the active course.

5. While attending a race event, stand far enough from the course to allow a racer on course full visibility, room to recover, and room to come to a stop without hitting you.

6. Always remain still while there is a racer on course, and never free-ski on or near a closed race course except as allowed by the established inspection procedures.

7. If a gate pole is knocked out or broken and presents a danger, place it outside the course, preferably totally to the side of the slope or as directed by the coaches. [*Author's note*: check the rules on reruns before doing this during a race.]

8. Be sure to communicate with your coach when tired, ill, uncertain, or afraid, if the course is too difficult or rough, or if visibility is poor.

9. Always stop below your coach or training group—never attempt to stop above any skier or group. Always leave room to take evasive action should your coach or others in your training group move unexpectedly.

10. When your run is complete, move immediately out of the finish area or away from the course. Make sure that you have an adequate finish area and safe room outside all courses.

11. Never jump or board fast into an uncontrolled blind spot.

12. When free-skiing outside race and training areas you must be aware of others and be in full control at all times. Respect other skiers'/snowboarders' rights to a safe and pleasant experience.

Martin Freinademetz racing at the U.S. Open. TREVOR GRAVES

Other Snowboarding Events

BoarderCross

Start with motocross, ditch the dirt and cycles, then add snow, snowboards, and a specialized set of rules and *voilà*, you've got BoarderCross! Boarder-Cross combines a little bit of everything— the thrills of freeriding, racing, and jumping; the intensity of head-to-head competition; and the joy of hanging with your friends. It is similar in spirit to skiing's "Chinese downhill"—an anything-goes race down the mountain—but BoarderCross adds strategically placed bumps, gates, and jumps to spice up the competition. Plus, this is the only event where riders compete against other riders shoulder to shoulder.

Since the first BoarderCross race at Blackcomb in the spring of 1991, these races have electrified spectators and riders alike. A standard course contains everything from washboards to jumps, banked turns to slalom gates. This puts alpine racers, freeriders, and freestylers on an equal footing, so the winners are the survivors with the best all-around riding skills.

An ideal BoarderCross event starts with 48 racers (preliminary rounds can be used to whittle down a larger pool of racers). Six racers ride head-to-head in each heat, with eight heats making up a round. Only the top half of the riders in each round advance to the next round, so there is a geometric regression from round to round (eight motos in round one, four motos in round two, two motos in round three, and only one moto in the final, or main, round).

On the course, the action is fast and close, especially as racers fight for position in the first gate. Light contact is expected as racers compete for the fastest line, but *obstruction fouls* are used to disqualify racers who intentionally veer from their course to bump, obstruct, or take out another racer. To prevent constant traffic jams, racers with the inside line (of the gates) are given the right of way. Still, passing is allowed anywhere on the course at any time.

From start to finish, few competitions pack more thrills and spills into a few minutes than BoarderCross. Even if you have no intention of ever entering one of these events, the experience of being there is one you won't want to miss.

Obstacle Courses

Obstacle courses are the latest craze in timed alpine racing. Obstacle courses contain jumps, quarterpipes, and wave sites. Riders descend the course one at a time and roar downhill as fast as they can.

Figure-Eight Competitions

Transport two snowboarders via helicopter or snow cat to the top of a virgin slope of powder, drop them off, then have them carve synchronized figure eights all the way back to the valley. That's a figure-eight competition. Scoring is based on the symmetry of the figure eights left in the path of the two snowboarders, and the synchronicity between the snowboarders themselves.

Banked Slalom

Take 26 slalom gates, place them in a deep, 200-yard-long gully (a creek bed in summer months), and you'll have the legendary Mt. Baker Banked Slalom. This demented twist on slalom racing makes for some of the most exciting alpine racing available.

Though the banked slalom closely resembles a typical slalom race, the steeply banked walls and elevated gates add new twists to the sport. Approach a gate near the top of the wall too slowly and you won't reach it; approach it too fast and you'll blow right out of the course! Although any ride down the course is fun, it takes a combination of halfpipe skills, racing skills, and guts to be a winner.

Extreme Competitions

Combine avalanches, cliffs, big airs, and the craziest freeriders in the universe and you have the World Extreme Championships. First held in 1992, in Valdez, Alaska, the World Extreme Championships give riders a chance to blow minds while doing what they do best—competing on some of the most extreme terrain imaginable.

The basic premise of an extreme competition is simple: toss a handful of fearless riders on wild, untamed terrain and see who performs best. There are no gates or designated lines—just insane displays of no-holds-barred freeriding.

With helicopters replacing chairlifts and snow cats, competitors are dropped off at the bottom of the mountain and given a chance to see the mountain from the judges' perspective. From there, the competitors pick out lines that they think will impress the judges, and spot landmarks to make the descent easier. The competitors then fly to the top of the mountain where they wait their turn. The riders descend one at a time and are judged on a scale of one to ten in six categories: *aggressiveness/attack*, *form/technique*, *fluidity*, *air*, *degree of difficulty/line of descent*, and *control*. Here's what each one means.

1. *Aggressiveness/attack*: The energy with which a boarder attacks or descends the chosen line.
2. *Form/technique*: The style with which a boarder attacks the chosen line.
3. *Fluidity*: The continuity, pace, and smoothness of transitions on the course.
4. *Air*: The style, poise, composure, and control with which a boarder executes airs, including takeoff, hang time, and landing.
5. *Degree of difficulty/line of descent*: The amount of exposure (read: *risk*) in the line of descent a boarder chooses.
6. *Control*: The degree of control exhibited during the descent. Any loss of control will result in a lower score. A fall is the ultimate loss of control; however, a skillful recovery will reduce the penalty. Lost equipment must be recovered before continuing a run.

While everyone gets caught up in the excitement of competing on extreme terrain, extreme competitions are meant to be fun. For mere mortals, the event looks pretty crazy. But to the riders themselves, it's a chance to push their personal envelopes. All in all, Matt Goodwill's comments following his first-place finish at the 1993 World Extreme Championships sum up every extreme rider's goals best: "Everyone did well because everybody lived, and that was the main goal."

Halfpipe Competitions

While alpine racers are trimming seconds off their race times, halfpipe competitors are pushing the limits of aerial showmanship in an attempt to get higher scores from a panel of judges. The atmosphere surrounding many halfpipe competitions is quite different than that at alpine races. There's loud music and specialized equipment, media stars and cutting-edge lingo. Make no mistake, however; the top halfpipe riders are also superb athletes. They train hard to perfect their tricks, and they know how to please judges. They mix elements of the athlete and the choreographer, the snowboarder and the acrobat—and put on a fascinating display every time.

As with alpine competitions, each competitor is responsible for knowing the rules used by the sanctioning organization. Get your hands on the entry form, rulebook, and competition guide and read them.

Judging Criteria

Depending on which organization sanctions the halfpipe competition, three to five judging criteria go into a competitor's overall score. The International Snowboard Federation rulebook outlines three criteria for scoring competitors: *amplitude*, *execution*, and *variety*. These are defined as follows:

1. *Amplitude*: The distance between the platform and the closest part of the racer and his equipment to the platform.
2. *Execution*: The fluent style of the jumps executed from the racer during the run without fault.

3. *Variety*: The total number of different maneuvers from the start to the finish of the run. Four different categories of maneuvers shall be presented in order to achieve the maximum points of variety. Those maneuvers consist of vertical rotation (i.e., inverted aerials), horizontal rotation (i.e., 180s and 540s), upright jumps (with hand grabs), and lip tricks (including handplants). To push your score even higher, you must complete those maneuvers both frontside and backside.

USSA uses five judging criteria in its halfpipe competitions: *amplitude, difficulty, landings, style,*

HALFPIPE TIPS

Most judges are looking for a unique ride. The best riders are willing to take some risks, but they stick their landings and make their tricks look easy. A mediocre trick can be made more spectacular by boning it out or tweaking harder than any other competitor. Pick a routine you're comfortable with, practice it, and have it totally choreographed in your mind. When it's your time to ride, ride like you own the pipe and play to the crowd. The judges are sure to increase your score.

—Scott Downey

Halfpipe competitions are exciting for competitors and spectators alike. PHOTO OF NICOLE ANGELRATH BY WARKOV, COURTESY BURTON SNOWBOARDS

A panel of judges watches keenly from the judging tent as halfpipe competitors vie for top finishes.

and *variety*. When there are three USSA judges, one judge is responsible for scoring amplitude, one for difficulty, and one for landings. All three judges also add a value for overall impression which includes the elements of *style* and *variety*. When five judges are used, each judge scores one category and no points are added for overall impression. The USSA rulebook defines each criterion as follows:

1. *Amplitude*: Amplitude represents the volume of execution, and is measured by the competitor's used energy. It is the degree of power and energy the competitor shows in the ride. This cate-gory deals with the height of maneuvers, the speed of the run, and the energy the competitor exhibits in an efficient manner.

2. *Difficulty*: The difficulty category represents the difficulty of the maneuver as well as the way that different maneuvers are put together to form the competitor's unique run. Many variables affect the difficulty, including the conditions and verticalness of the pipe, the height at which the trick is performed, the grab used, whether the trick is toeside or heelside, the number of maneuvers performed fakie, the degree of spin, etc. The important consideration for the judge of the difficulty category is to evaluate maneuvers in relationship to the overall run.

3. *Landings*: Landings in a run are determined by analyzing the competitor's balance, precision, stability, and rhythm. Items that deduct from the overall score are dragging hands, flailing arms, stopping in the halfpipe, and falling. The landings judge shall evaluate the run from landings and across the bottom of the pipe. Other factors include recovers, the use of the transition, spin-outs, and flailing. Falls that occur are a 25 percent deduction for each fall, but are only assessed by the landings judge.

4. *Style*: Style is increased by accentuating the maneuver. This is done by smooth, powerful riding as demonstrated by holding the grabs, boning, and tweaking. Style is decreased by falling, flailing, or the failure to enhance the maneuver.

5. *Variety*: Variety is expressed by doing more maneuvers, different maneuvers, and more maneuvers of different types. This includes handplants, riding fakie, aerials, etc., in which a high degree of variety is shown to the judges.

VISUALIZATION

Mental imagery can really help in competitions. Whether I'm racing or riding the halfpipe, I first try to run everything through in my mind. In racing events, you're usually allowed a visual inspection by walking or sideslipping the course first. If I can do that, I'll memorize the course, then picture myself racing through every turn. If it's going to be a 30- or 40-second race, I'll take a full 30 or 40 seconds to run it through in my mind.

In halfpipe competitions, you're usually allowed some practice sessions. So before the event starts, I'll get down a basic run that I know I can do well. I'll memorize, plan, and choreograph each individual hit, then I'll do the same thing I did in racing: I'll stretch out, take a few breaths, close my eyes, and imagine the entire ride in real time. I'll picture where I'm going to pump off a wall, where I'm going to land, and what it will all feel like.

Taking your time to visualize and imagine every detail is the best way for your mind to fully get a run dialed in. But if you just do a quick memory check, you may rush your ride—even miss a gate or trick—because you forget the details.

—*Craig Kelly, four-time World Champion*

Slopestyle Competitions

Slopestyle events are among the most dynamic of the freestyle competitions. A typical slopestyle course can contain quarterpipes, spines, and waves, plus obstacles like rails, boxes, and logs.

Like the halfpipe competitions, slopestyle competitions are displays of riding ability and showmanship. Competitors can take any route they choose through the slopestyle course and can mix slides, spins, bonks, and ollies in any combination. The winners use all of the obstacles and a wide variety of tricks to come up with the best freestyle routine.

10 Built to Last
Tuning and Maintenance

Dull edges can lead to a little hard luck in turns . . . even at the U.S. Open. PHOTO OF JASEY ANDERSON BY DENNIS CURRAN/SPORTS FILE

Whether you're a recreational snowboarder or a professional racer, there's nothing quite so exhilarating as riding a well-tuned snowboard. Properly tuned snowboards do what you want them to do. They turn easily, slide smoothly, and bite well in hard snow.

If you are a recreational snowboarder, this translates into a faster learning curve. Your tuned board won't take off in the wrong direction or hook edges while you're trying to turn. If you are a racer, tuning will make you go faster and help you improve your standings. Freestyle riders benefit from specialized tuning tricks that make sliding and spinning easier.

The word *tuning* can conjure fear in recreational snowboarding circles since many snowboarders think of edge tuning, base repair, and hot waxing as mystical arts, practiced behind closed doors in the secret recesses of local board shops.

But as you'll soon find out, tuning is easy and fun. In this chapter, we will demystify snowboard maintenance and repair, and teach you step-by-step how to take care of your own equipment. Then, next time you hit the slopes, you'll see how dramatically tuning changes the way both you and your board ride.

Shop Repairs

Home tuning and repair work can take care of things like minor base repairs, edge filing, and waxing. However, some repairs—such as leveling concave bases—are best left to your shop technician.

A few repair problems that should prompt a visit to your local shop are *delamination* and *deep gouges*. If your board's base, deck, or edges begin to delaminate, hand the repair work over to your shop technician. He can rebuild your board or talk to you about obtaining a replacement model. Base gouges that extend into the core can shorten your board's life dramatically if they're not repaired promptly. Have your shop fill them in as soon as possible.

Tools of the Trade

It takes only a handful of basic tools and materials to do your own tuning and repairs. You can find most of these materials at your local board shop. Some of the tools—such as files and Scotchbrite pads—can be found in hardware stores. Here's a list of items you ought to have:

- base cleaner
- bastard files, 6-, 8-, and 12-inch mill
- brushes, brass and nylon
- edge file
- electric iron or hot wax machine
- fiberline paper or lint-free cloth
- file brush or card
- file holder
- plastic scraper
- polishing stones, carborundum, Arkansas, ceramic, or diamond
- P-Tex candles
- rubber stone (gummi stone)

With just a handful of readily available tools, you can keep your snowboarding equipment properly tuned for all types of riding conditions.

- sandpaper (silicon carbide or emery), 100, 120, 180, and 220 grit
- scrubbing pads, Fibertex or Scotchbrite
- stainless steel scraper
- tuning bar
- wax
- waxing cork

The Five Basic Steps

This chapter breaks snowboard tuning down into five easy steps: *edge filing, base preparation, base repair, base structuring,* and *waxing.* Each step deals with just one part of the board or tuning problem, but they all work together to get your snowboard completely tuned and ready to ride.

Step One: Edge Filing

Edges help you initiate turns and grip the snow. If edges are in good shape, they'll hold tight and provide a solid platform. But if they're rounded or burred, they'll slip free and make turning difficult. In this section, you'll learn how to keep the edges properly tuned for a variety of situations, and how to keep them sharp all day long.

Every snowboard edge can be broken down into two parts: the *base edge* and the *side edge.* The

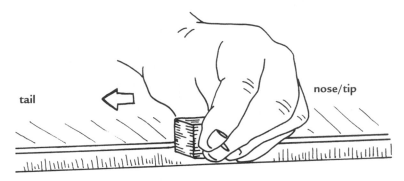

Use carborundum, Arkansas, ceramic, or diamond stones to polish your edges to a smooth finish. Place the stone flush against each edge and drag it from tip to tail. The stone will smooth out nicks and burrs. Stones are also handy for touching up your edges after each day of riding.

easiest way to care for both edges is to maintain them daily with a carborundum stone or diamond stone. Place the stone flush against each edge and drag it from tip to tail. The stone will smooth out nicks and burrs and return your edges to freshly tuned condition. Another couple of passes over the edge with a rubber stone will polish the edges to a luster. Though stones are good for edge maintenance, filing may be the only way to restore the edges to their original sharpness.

Starting with the base edge, push or drag (whichever feels more comfortable) a 6- or 8-inch mill bastard file over the entire length of the base edge. Keep it parallel with the base to cut a 0-degree edge, but be careful not to file the base itself. Use smooth, even strokes working from tip to tail so that you remove the same amount of material from both base edges. (Don't saw back and forth. Sawing can dull the file and grind filings into the base.)

Sometimes you'll feel your file skip over part of an edge. That's because collisions with rocks and hard objects harden the steel edge. Rough these areas up with a stone, and you'll have no problem getting your file to bite. Once you're done filing the base edge, use a whetstone to polish the edges smooth.

File the side edge next. Side edges can be a little trickier for two reasons. First, the board's sidecut gets in the way of larger files. A specially designed edge file simplifies filing preset edge angles. Or, you can use a 6- to 8-inch mill bastard file. Second, the narrow sidewall makes it hard to judge a 90-degree angle.

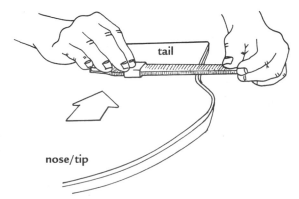

*File the **base edge** with a 6- or 8-inch **bastard file**. Work from the tip to the tail using smooth, even strokes.*

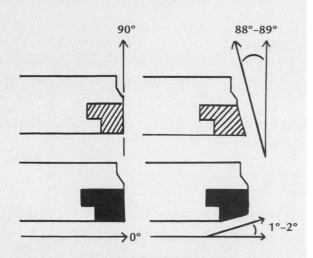

An exaggerated look at **beveled edges**.

EDGE BEVELING

Most new boards come with edges ground at 0 degrees (base edge) and 90 degrees (side edge). With the help of adjustable file guides and file holders you can change these angles and alter the way your snowboard rides.

Increasing the base edge angle from 0 to 1 or 2 degrees decreases your snowboard's grip on the snow. At the same time, it speeds up your glide and increases the ease of turning. (This is helpful for slalom racers and freestyle riders alike.)

Decreasing the side edge angle from 90 to 89 or 88 degrees increases the snowboard's ability to grip the snow and makes turning easier in icy conditions.

There are many ways to combine base and side edge angles. A board with a 1-degree base angle and 89 degrees of side angle may pivot, slide, and edge better for you. Start conservatively with your adjustments (you don't want to file away too much edge) and try different combinations until you find what you like best.

—*David Sher, Mountain and Surf Pro Shop, Sacramento, California*

Most snowboarders get around this by using a file holder that presets the file angle.

File side edges the same way you filed the base edge. Use long, even strokes to remove an even amount of material, file the entire edge, and finish the job by polishing the edges with a stone.

The last step in edge-tuning is to take a Scotchbrite pad and dull or *detune* the tip and tail edges beyond the effective edge. Detuning prevents the edges from catching when you're gliding straight or from hooking too early at the start of a turn.

There are many ways to detune your snowboard. Start by thoroughly detuning the edges on the tip and tail shovels by rubbing them with the Scotchbrite pad. (You only want to remove the sharp edge, not file the edges round.) Next, detune 3 to 6 inches of the effective edge from the front of the effective edge (near the tip) back toward your feet. Finally, detune 1 to 3 inches of the effective edge nearest the tail. Using this detuning pattern as a starting point, you can detune more or less of the effective edge to suit your riding style.

There are two tricks to make filing fun and easy. First, paint the entire length of each edge with a black magic marker to help guide your progress. Your filing is complete when the black marks are gone. Second, keep your file and base clean. Use a

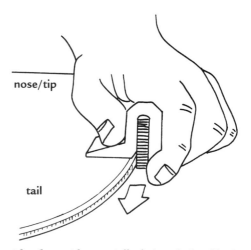

File the **side edges** *with a specially designed* **edge file**. *An edge file is easier to use and simplifies filing preset edge angles. As with base edge filing, work from tip to tail with long, smooth, even strokes. If you don't have an edge file, use a 6- to 8-inch mill bastard file.*

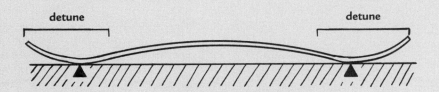

DETUNING

Detuning prevents your edges from catching when gliding or from hooking too early in your turn. Detune your edges to match your style of riding. If you like to spin a lot, try detuning all the way to the outside of your feet, keeping only the edges between your feet sharp. If you plan to slide rails or logs, you can completely detune your edges to keep them from snagging.

Alpine riders can detune their edges asymmetrically even if they're riding a symmetrical board. Starting with the tip of the snowboard, detune a little less on the toe edge and a little more on the heel edge. When you get to the tail, detune more on the toe edge and less on the heel edge. When you're done, the center of the tuned sections will be more forward on your toe edge than on your heel edge.

There's no right or wrong way to detune your edges. Experiment with different detuning patterns, find what feels best to you, and stick with it.

—Scott Downey

---

file brush or file card to clean metal from the file, and use fiberline or a clean rag to wipe filings from the base.

Step Two: Base Preparation

There are two necessary steps in base preparation: remove old wax and dirt, and check the base for levelness.

There are two ways to clean bases. The easiest way is to spray or flood the base with *base cleaner/wax remover*. This is a special solvent that dissolves wax and draws impurities to the surface. Let the solvent sit on the base for a couple of minutes, then wipe it off with fiberline or a lint-free cloth. Base cleaners can give off heavy, toxic fumes, so work in a well-ventilated area and wear rubber gloves to protect your hands. Once you're done cleaning the base, let the board air out for fifteen or twenty minutes before doing any repairs. This will let any residual base cleaner evaporate.

The second way to clean bases is to *hot wax* and *scrape* the base before the wax has a chance to cool. With this method, the heat draws out the dirt and old wax, while the scraper takes it off the base. If you want to try this technique, flip forward to the section on hot waxing, but remember to scrape off the wax before it has a chance to cool.

If the base is extremely dirty, it may take two or three cleansings before it's clean. Once the base is clean, check it for levelness by rolling a *true bar* down its entire length. The true bar—a perfectly round steel dowel—will highlight problem areas by letting light shine between the base and the true bar. (If you don't have a true bar, use a ruler or some other straight edge.) Note any gouges or protrusions so you can level these off when you start repairing the base.

Curved bases are difficult to fix at home. A concave base (indented in the middle) puts too much edge on the snow, which may cause the snowboard to hook or veer at random. The opposite of a concave base is a convex base (bulged in the middle). Convex bases swim or float on the snow, making it harder to glide straight or hold an edge.

Snowboards can be specially tuned to meet all types of conditions, from halfpipes to powder, and from spring crud to winter ice. PHOTO OF J. J. COLLIER BY ROB GRACIE

If you have problems with either convex or concave bases, take your board to a shop and have them even out the base and edges. Concave bases can be cured by filing the edges down to the point where they're level with the base. Convex bases are corrected by sanding the base down until it's even with the edges.

Step Three: Base Repair

Scratches, gouges, and protrusions in the base act like tiny rudders that can give the board a mind of its own. Filling or shaving these imperfections will help return your board to a straight, true path and will improve its gliding performance significantly.

Begin your base repairs by removing protrusions or pushed up sections of the base with a steel

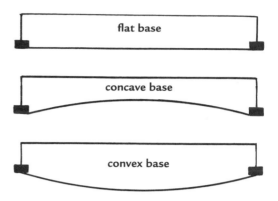

If you have problems with either convex or concave bases, take your board to a shop and have the bases and edges evened out. Concave bases are corrected by filing the edges down to the point where they're level with the base. Convex bases are corrected by sanding the base down until it's even with the edges.

scraper. Carefully slice away the lifted base until it's even with the adjoining base.

Next, fill in gouges with a *P-Tex candle*—a drip-repair candle that is made of paraffin and polyethylene plastic. (The candle drips molten polyethylene into the gouges, and the excess is scraped away after it cools.) Light the candle with a lighter or regular candle. Once it starts to burn, hold it close over a metal scraper until you notice a low, blue flame. Anytime the candle starts to turn brown or black, too much carbon is forming. Since carbon interferes with the adhesion of the P-Tex, it must be minimized. Do this by holding the candle closer to the scraper, or by twisting the candle against the scraper to wipe off the carbon build-up.

Hold the candle within an inch of the base and let the P-Tex drip into the gouge, building it up just enough so that it is raised above the surrounding base. If the gouge is very deep or wide, fill it in a little bit at a time, working from tail to tip. (That way, the scale pattern will deflect snow rather than catch it.) You can even use the steel scraper to push the liquid P-Tex into hard-to-reach crevices.

Once you've filled in all the gouges, let the P-Tex cool to room temperature, then use the steel scraper to remove the excess material. Start in the center of the repair, and scrape toward the edges. Make your last few passes with the steel scraper from tip to tail.

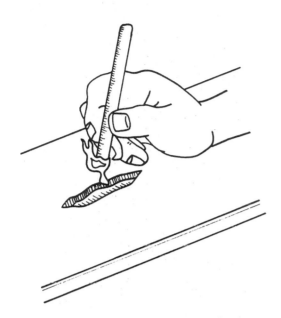

P-Tex candles are used to fill in small gouges in your base. Light the candle with a propane torch or butane lighter, and hold a steel scraper near the flame to keep the flame small and blue. Drip the P-Tex into the gouge a little bit at a time in overlapping scales. When you're done, use a steel scraper to shave away the excess P-Tex.

P-Tex repairs are quick and easy, but they're not foolproof: P-Tex doesn't stick as well to hard, sintered polyethylene bases; isn't great for large, deep gouges; and may not provide the level of performance some racers need. If you fit into these categories, consider bringing your snowboard to a shop and getting the base work done professionally. They can use extruders and base welders, which work at higher temperatures (300°F–500°F) and make stronger repairs. (These tools allow solid repairs, but the higher temperatures can damage the base if the tools are not used correctly.) Your shop repair person may even be willing to show you how to use base welding tools so that you can make advanced repairs on your own.

Step Four: Base Structuring

After you finish with base repairs, you can texture or *structure* the base so that it will glide well over the snow. Structuring is putting a finely grooved pattern into the base in order to cut down on the drag-ging effects of friction and suction. The micro-grooves allow air and water to pass under the base without slowing your snowboard down.

There are three ways to structure a base: *sanding*, *using a riller bar*, and *brushing*.

To sand structure into your base, use sandpaper made of silicon carbide or emery. Wrap the paper around a sanding block and use smooth overlapping strokes that extend from tip to tail (never sand from tail to nose). Sand the base three times—first with 100-grit paper, then with 120-grit paper, and finally with 180-grit. If it is very cold (below 15°F), sand a fourth time with 220-grit paper. If it is warmer (above 32°F), stop sanding at 120-grit paper.

After sanding, polish the base from tip to tail with Scotchbrite or Fibertex abrasive pads. Next, brush the base with a soft brass brush. Finally, polish the base one last time with the Scotchbrite. This will leave a clean, structured base free of any excess fibers.

Riller bars—special tools with small teeth similar to those of a file—make for cleaner, easier structuring because they indent the base instead of tearing it. Use the side of the riller bar with fine teeth for cold conditions, and the side with coarse teeth for warmer conditions. Hold the riller bar against the base at a 45-degree angle and push or pull it from tip to tail. After one or two passes, polish the base with an abrasive pad to smooth and remove any fibers.

Specially designed steel-bristled brushes provide the final method for structuring. Aggressively

P-TEX CANDLES

After you're done with a P-Tex candle, blow it out and twist off the remaining molten material with the steel scraper. Don't reuse the burned part of a P-Tex candle. It has already been altered chemically by the heat and will not bond as well with the base. If you didn't get a chance to twist off the burned part of the candle, cut the candle back a quarter inch before you use it again.

—*Scott Downey*

brush the base with short, overlapping, back-and-forth strokes. Next, brush the base a couple more times from tip to tail. Finally, polish the base from tip to tail with the abrasive pad.

Step Five: Waxing

Waxing is the easiest and most common of all tuning jobs. It produces immediate results. Since wax makes it easier for snowboards to glide over snow, a waxed board will slide faster and turn easier. Waxing also protects the base from the harmful effects of moisture, UV rays, snow contaminants, and dirt.

Recreational snowboarders can wax their boards before every trip, if they're ambitious. Professional competitors invariably wax their boards to match the snow conditions. If you're an average snowboarder, try waxing your board every two or three times that you go snowboarding, and more often if you're riding on icy snow. Some spray or wipe-on waxes can even be carried in your pocket and applied on the slope.

Before waxing your board, make sure that you've already completed step one (cleaning the base). The base must be clean before it will accept wax well.

You need only three things to wax your board: *wax*, an *iron* (or waxing machine), and a *plastic scraper*. Using either a waxing iron or an old steamless iron, hold a bar of wax against the base of the iron and let the wax drip onto the base. Run a bead of wax back and forth along the base without ever letting the iron touch the base. The iron should be hot enough to melt the wax, but not so hot that the wax smokes. (About 250°F is normal.)

Once the wax has been applied along the entire length of the base, smooth it out with the iron, being careful not to let the iron stall or touch the plastic base. Spread a thin layer of wax evenly over the entire base (if the iron doesn't glide smoothly, there's not enough wax on the base).

While the wax is cooling to room temperature, sharpen your plastic scraper with a 12-inch mill bastard file. Lay the file flat on a table and drag the thin edge of the scraper over it. Keep the scraper at 90 degrees to the file, and file until the scraper's edge is smooth and sharp.

Once the wax has completely cooled (this can take 20 to 30 minutes), scrape off the excess wax

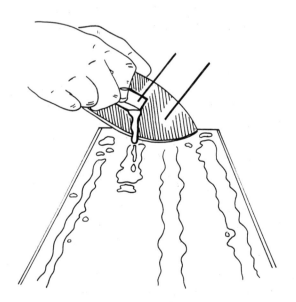

Using either a waxing iron or an old steamless iron, hold a bar of wax against the base of the iron and let the wax drip onto the base. Run a bead of wax back and forth along the base without ever letting the iron touch the base. The iron should be hot enough to melt the wax, but not so hot that the wax smokes.

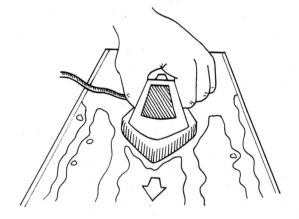

Once the wax has been applied along the entire length of the base, carefully smooth it out with the iron, being careful not to let the iron stall or touch the plastic. Spread a thin layer of wax evenly over the entire base.

by pushing or pulling the scraper from tip to tail. Some snowboarders like to put some finishing touches on their wax jobs. One technique is to buff the remaining wax with a waxing cork (this improves performance below 15°F). For the best results, use a soft nylon brush for cold conditions, and a soft bronze brush for warm conditions. Brushing the base briskly with small, quick strokes until there are no more little white balls of wax helps the board glide faster. Finally, polishing the base lightly with an abrasive pad can make riding smoother and more enjoyable. Whatever you do, make sure to scrape excess wax from the steel edges so they can cut into the snow, and go have fun!

Deck and Sidewall Repairs

Little chips, splits, or gouges in the deck and side-walls don't necessarily affect a snowboard's performance. However, moisture can seep in through the gouges and cause delaminations or lead to deterioration in the core.

Minor deck and sidewall repairs are a breeze. Just get some two-part epoxy from your local hobby shop, mix the parts together, and apply the epoxy to the gouge. If the top sheet or sidewall is starting to delaminate, use two or more C-clamps and a block of wood to firmly press the loose material into the epoxy. Once it's dry, the board will be as good as new. Major gouges should be repaired by a shop technician. If the snowboard is delaminating without any evidence of riding damage, call the dealer or manufacturer to see if it is covered in the warranty.

Customizing Your Bindings

Many snowboarders customize their strap, step-in, and plate bindings so that they match their boot size and riding style. Customization improves the way your boot and binding fit. In turn, it improves your safety and comfort level while making it easier to ride like you want to.

If you can rotate the highbacks on your strap and step-in highback bindings, turn them until they're parallel with the snowboard's heel edge. This will give you more control when carving heel-side turns (your ankles will hit the heelbacks whenever you lean back) and increase your flexibility (the heelbacks won't be in your way when you're boning tricks).

Next, if your highbacks are interchangeable, pick one that matches your riding style. Use taller,

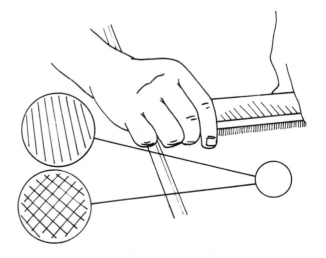

Once the wax is completely cooled, scrape off the excess by pushing or pulling a scraper from tip to tail. Always tilt the top of the scraper in the direction you're scraping to ensure that the scraper won't cut into the base.

After you're done waxing, brushing the base briskly using small, quick strokes until there are no more little white balls of wax helps the board glide faster. For the best results, use a soft nylon brush for cold conditions, and a soft bronze brush for warm conditions. If the snow is new and cold, use parallel strokes. Crisscross your strokes for warmer, wetter snow.

CHECK YOUR HARDWARE

Your snowboard, bindings, and boots are put under immense torque and stress when you are riding. All that pressure inevitably loosens the very screws and bolts that hold your bindings together. So, every day before you take your snowboard out on the hill, take the time to thoroughly inspect and tighten your equipment. Check every screw and bolt on your board. Be sure to tighten up any binding screws or strap bolts that have loosened during previous use and you'll ride much safer.

—*Charles Arnell*

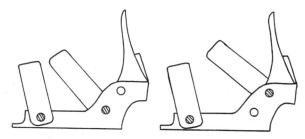

*Adjust your **strap placement** to match your riding style. The heel strap is mounted lower on the binding on the left so that it comes down across the rider's arch. (That opens up your foot movement and makes it easier to bone tricks.) The heel strap on the right is mounted higher so that it rides higher on the rider's arch and back toward the heel. (That holds your heel down better and makes the board more stable when you're cranking it up on edge.)*

cup-shaped heelbacks for carving, and shorter, flatter highbacks for freestyle and halfpipe riding.

If you use strap bindings, you can adjust your strap placement to match your riding style. If you spend most of your time carving turns, position the ankle strap higher on your arch and back toward your heel. That will hold your heel down better and make the board more stable when you're cranking it up on edge. If you're spending more time in the halfpipe or doing freestyle tricks, mount the heel strap lower so that it comes down across your arch. That will open up your foot movement and make it easier to bone tricks.

Some step-in bindings have internal highbacks in the boots. These boots have special adjustment points that allow riders to stiffen or soften the flex of the internal highback. Follow the manufacturer's directions and adjust the highback to suit your riding style. Other step-ins have external highbacks attached to the bindings. These external highbacks can be adjusted the same way as highbacks used in traditional strap bindings.

The most important adjustment to plate bindings is your boot-size adjustment. The bails should be set so that they firmly grip the boot's heel and toe protrusions without risk of popping loose. Also, many hard boots have adjustable flexes that let you dial in the correct flex and stiffness for your weight, ability, and intended terrain use. Just follow each manufacturer's directions for these adjustments.

Toe Ramps

Some strap bindings incorporate toe ramps (also known as gas pedals) into the binding designs. These ramps curve upward in the toe area, following the natural upward curve on the toe of the boot. Toe ramps are designed to quickly transmit toe pressure to the toe edge. This action is often called "step-

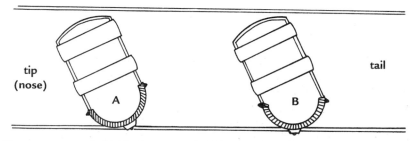

tip (nose)   A   B   tail

If you can rotate the highbacks on your highback bindings, turn them until they're parallel with the snowboard's heel edge. That will give you more control when carving heelside turns and will increase your flexibility.

pin' on the gas," hence the gas-pedal nickname. These performance-oriented toe ramps may also help riders with exceptionally large feet. The toe ramp can help lift the boot toe off the snow slightly higher than a binding without toe ramps. There are trade-offs for the extra toe-edge power and toe lift, however, since toe ramps may make your feet feel more fatigued at the end of a run.

Cants and Wedges

Cants and wedges are shims that mount between the bindings and snowboard. They work with all types of bindings and can help improve your riding by tilting your feet to naturalize your stance.

Cants—or cant plates—lift your heels higher than your toes, or vice versa. Many racers cant both feet, lifting their back heel and their front toes. This makes it easier to drive your knees together, flex the board, and carve turns. However, you can cant your feet any way that works for you.

Wedges—or bevel plates—tilt the outside of your foot toward the arch. When used on the back foot, wedges drive your back knee into the pocket behind your front knee. Once again, this naturalizes your stance and makes carving easier.

Many modern cants mix wedges and cants in one unit. For example, a cant for your back foot can lift your heel above your toes and tilt your foot toward the tip of the snowboard. Ask your local shop rep what will work with your board. You might

Roof racks are a safe and secure way to transport your boards to the mountain. BRANDI EASTER, COURTESY YAKIMA

find that cants give you that extra bit of leverage you need to make your riding skills and your snowboard come together as one unit.

Transporting Your Snowboard

Now that you've spent all this time tuning and maintaining your snowboard, why would you let it rattle around an airplane baggage compartment or subject it to road salt on the way to the mountain? Transporting your board in a specially designed padded snowboard bag will save it from wear and tear wherever you go. The bag will protect the edges, base, deck, and sidewalls from chips and dents. When traveling to the mountain, lock your board tightly in a specially designed roof rack so that it doesn't bang around in the back of the car.

SUMMERTIME SNOWBOARDING

If you ride at one of the few areas open to snowboarding all summer long, you'll encounter snow conditions rarely found any other time of the year. Salt—which is often added to the snow to prolong its life and improve its texture—grinds against your base as you ride. At the same time, intense ultraviolet rays and heat break down the rest of your gear and shorten its life.

Wash off all your gear with fresh water after a day on the slopes, and keep your board well-waxed. Some snowboarders carry around a bar of

soap to rub on the base instead of wax. Soap cuts down on time spent hot-waxing your board, and works as long as you keep reapplying it. Do your best to keep your edges tuned, but don't bevel them very much. The salt and dirt in the snow will do that for you automatically.

When you're done snowboarding for the summer, wax your board and store it away until winter. The wax will protect the board and get it ready for the winter season. All you have to do then is take it out of storage, scrape off the wax, and go riding.

—Scott Downey

APPENDIX

Snowboarding Checklist

It's easy to leave your hat, goggles, or gloves at home when you're anxious to go out riding. Here's a handy checklist to make sure all your important gear makes it to the mountain with you.

- bindings
- boots
- gloves
- goggles
- hat
- leash
- lip balm
- lift ticket
- money
- parka
- polishing stone
- repair tools
- snowboard
- snowboard pants
- socks
- stomp pad
- sunblock
- sweater
- thermal underwear
- wax

Backcountry Checklist

The basics: first-aid kit, compass, map, sunblock, extra clothing, food, water, protective eyewear.

Optional equipment: snowshoes, crampons, collapsible poles, ice ax, shovels, avalanche transceivers, backpack.

Snowboarding Camps

Most ski areas offer snowboarding instruction, including group lessons, private lessons, and specialized camps. Call your favorite resort to see what's available. The camps listed below also provide an excellent way to tune your snowboarding skills.

Camp of Champions
2713 Sproat Drive
Whistler BC V0N 1B2
Canada
888-997-CAMP (888-997-2267)
www.campofchampions.com

Chill
The Burton Foundation
P.O. Box 4458
Burlington VT 05406

802-651-0326
www.burton.com
Chill is a nonprofit learn-to-snowboard program for underprivileged and at-risk youth.

Delaney Adult Snowboarding Camps
4876 Sterling Drive
Boulder CO 80301
800-743-3790
www.delaneysnowboarding.com

Freestyle Camp
Stowe Mountain Resort
5781 Mountain Rd.
Stowe VT 05672
802-253-3500
www.stowe.com/school/snowboarding

High Cascade Snowboard Camp
P.O. Box 6622
Bend OR 97708
800-334-4272; 541-389-7404
www.highcascade.com

Mike Jacoby/Grand Targhee Ski & Summer Resort
P.O. Box Ski
Alta WY 83422
307-353-2300; 800-TARGEE (800-827-4433)
www.grandtarghee.com

Mt. Hood Snowboard Camp
P.O. Box 140
Rhododendron OR 97049
800-247-5552
www.snowboardcamp.com

Northwest Snowboard Training Center
25815 Mountain Drive
Arlington WA 98223
360-435-9718
www.tgi.net/nwsnowboard

Transworld Snowboarding
www.tsnow.com/directories/camps.html
A directory with contact information for national and international camps.

U.S. Snowboard Training Center
P.O. Box 360
Brightwood OR 97011
800-325-4430
www.snowboardtraining.com

Dave Murray Whistler Summer Ski and Snow-
    board Camp
103-4338 Main Street, Suite 981
Whistler BC V0N 1B4
Canada
604-932-0565
www.skiandsnowboard.com

Whistler Summer Snowboard Camps
103-4338 Main St., Suite 981
Whistler BC V0N 1B4
Canada
604-932-0565
www.whistlersnowboardcamps.com

Wild Women Snowboarding Camp
c/o Oxygen Media
75 9th Ave., 8th Floor
New York NY 10011
877-SHE-RIPS (877-743-7477)
www.wildwomencamps.com

Windell's Snowboard Camp
P.O. Box 628
Welches OR 97067
800-765-7669
www.windells.com

Women's Snowboard Clinics
Whitetail Resort
13805 Blairs Valley Rd.
Mercersburg PA 17326
717-328-9400
www.skiwhitetail.com

Women Only Snowboard Camps
c/o Katie Bush
P.O. Box 766
Waitsfield VT 05673
800-451-4574
www.snowevents.com

Snowboarding Magazines

Snowboarder
P.O. Box 1028
Dana Point CA 92629
949-496-5922
www.snowboardermag.com

Snowboarding
Snowboard Life

353 Airport Rd.
Oceanside CA 92054-1203
760-722-7777; 800-788-7072
www.snowboarding-online.com

Magazines with Occasional Snowboarding Articles

Couloir, The Backcountry Snowboard and Ski
    Magazine
P.O. Box 2349
Truckee CA 96160
530-582-1884
www.couloir-mag.com

Mountainfreak
P.O. Box 4149
Telluride CO 81435
970-728-9731
www.mountainfreak.com

Powder
P.O. Box 1028
Dana Point CA 92629
949-496-5922
www.powdermag.com

Ski
Skiing
P.O. Box 55533
Boulder CO 80322
303-448-7600; 800-678-0817; 800-825-5552
www.skinet.com

Ski Racing International
P.O. Box 1125
Waitsfield VT 05673
802-496-7700
www.skiracing.com

Winter Sport Business
502 West Cordova Road.
Santa Fe NM 87501
505-986-1257
www.wintersportbiz.com

Useful Websites

10feet.com, www.10feet.com
Abysmal Snowboarding, www.snowboarding.as
'boarderLine, www.theboarderline.com
Boarding.com, www.boarding.com
BoardSnow.com, www.boardsnow.com
boardtheworld, www.boardtheworld.com
Boardz.com, www.boards.com/snowboard
Female Riders Club, www.femaleridersclub.com
Heckler, www.heckler.com
Hyperski, www.hyperski.com

MountainZone.com, www.mountainzone.com/
   snowboarding
Original Gimp Adaptive Snowboarding, www.
   originalgimp.org
Skate-Snow Network, www.thessn.com
Ski Central, www.skicentral.com
Snowboarding.com, www.snowboarding.com
Snowboarding-Online.com, www.
   solsnowboarding.com
SnowboardingTips.com, www.
   snowboardingtips.com
SnowBoardNW.com, www.snowboardnw.com
Snwbrdr Online, www.snwbrdronline.com
Transworld Snowboarding, www.tsnow.com

Trade Associations

National Ski Areas Association
133 South Van Gordon Street, Suite 300
Lakewood CO 80228
303-987-1111
www.nsaa.org

National Ski and Snowboard Retailers Association
1601 Feehanville Dr., Suite 300
Mt. Prospect IL 60056-6035
847-391-9825
www.nssra.com

Snow Sports Association for Women
4261 Piedra Place
Boulder CO 80301
305-545-6882
www.snowlink.com

SnowSports Industries America
8377-B Greensboro Drive
McLean VA 22102
703-556-9020
www.snowlink.com, www.snowsports.org

Washington Ski and Snowboard Industries
P.O. Box 2325
Seattle WA 98111-2325
206-623-3777
www.skiindustry.com/wssi

Snowboarding Organizations

There are many organizations that sanction and sponsor
competitions. Keep in mind that snowboarding is young,
and that these organizations may change. You can keep
track of them by reading snowboarding magazines or by
getting a list of events held at major ski resorts.

American Association of Snowboard Instructors
133 South Van Gordon Street, Suite 100
Lakewood CO 80228

303-987-2700
www.aasi.org

Canadian Snowboard Federation
88 Canada Olympic Road, S.W.
Calgary AB T3B 5R5
Canada
403-202-1015
www.csf.ca

International Snowboard Federation (ISF), North
   America
315 East Alcott Avenue
Fergus Falls MN 56537
218-739-4843
www.isf.ch

Professional Snowboarders Association of North
   America (PSA)
P.O. Box 477
Vail CO 81658

United States of America Snowboard Association
   (USASA)
P.O. Box 3927
Truckee CA 96160
800-404-9213
www.usasa.org

United States Ski and Snowboard Association
   (USSA)
P.O. Box 100
Park City UT 84060
435-649-9090
www.usskiteam.com
www.ussnowboard.com

Utah Ski and Snowboard Association/Ski
   Utah
150 W. 500 S.
Salt Lake City UT 84101
801-534-1779; 800-SKI-UTAH (800-754-8824)
www.skiutah.com

Other Snowboarding Organizations

International Ski Federation (FIS),
   www.fis-ski.com
International Snowboard Federation, Asia (ISF
   Asia), www.isf.ch
International Snowboard Federation, Europe (ISF
   Europe), www.isf.ch
Japan Snowboarding Association (JSBA),
   www.so-net.ne.jb.jsba
Professional Snowboarders Association of Asia
   (PSA Asia), www.psa-a.gr.jp
Snowboard Australia
   www.snowboardaustralia.org.au

Halfpipe Specifications

The *International Snowboard Federation* and *USSA* are two of the largest sanctioning bodies for halfpipe competitions. The table below shows the specifications of halfpipes used in competitions held by these organizations.

HALFPIPE SPECIFICATIONS

Halfpipe Specifications	International Snowboarding Federation	USSA
Inclination	11 to 24 degrees	20 degrees
Length	50 to 110 meters	100 meters
Width from wall to wall	10 to 18 meters	15 meters
Inner height of walls	1.5 to 3 meters	2 meters
Transition radius	1.5 to 3 meters	2 meters
Vertical	10 to 30 cm	20 cm
Platform width	1 meter minimum	1 meter minimum
Entry ramp	2 meters or less	2 meters

HALFPIPE TRICK CHART: FRONTSIDE WALL

	Front Hand Toe Edge	Front Hand Heel Edge	Back Hand Toe Edge	Back Hand Heel Edge
Near Nose	Slob	Frontside Method	Crail (bone back leg)	Nuclear
Between Bindings	Slob	Melanchollie	frontside air	Stale Fish (reach around back leg) or Reverse (reach around front leg)
Near Tail	Beginner's Seatbelt	Walt air	///////////	Beginner's Stale Fish
Through Legs to Opposite Edge	Tai Pan	Stalemasky	Canadian Bacon	Roast Beef (bone back leg) or Chicken Salad (bone front leg)
On Tail	Seatbelt		Tail Grab	

HALFPIPE TRICK CHART: BACKSIDE WALL

	Front Hand Toe Edge	Front Hand Heel Edge	Back Hand Toe Edge	Back Hand Heel Edge
Near Nose	Mute air (if you tweak it, it's a Japan air)	backside air	Backside Crail	Nuclear
Between Bindings	Mute Air	Method air (board goes above your head) or Palmer (board goes out to side)	Indy Air	Fresh Fish (reach around back leg) or Reverse (reach around front leg)
Near Tail	Beginner's Seatbelt	Walt air	Tail Snatch	Beginner's Fresh Fish
Through Legs to Opposite Edge	Tai Pan	Stalemasky	Canadian Bacon	Roast Beef (bone back leg) or Chicken Salad (bone front leg)
On Tail	Seatbelt		Tail Grab	

A FEW WORDS ABOUT THESE TRICKS: The trick chart is just a starting point for halfpipe tricks. It doesn't always tell you which leg to bone, when to arch your back, or which way to twist your waist. However, the more time you spend in the halfpipe, the more likely you are to learn the finer points of each trick. Also, if the riders in your region call a trick by a different name, that's all right. A trick is just a trick. Don't get hung up on a name—just have fun!

Glossary

Aerial: A flip done off the wall of a half-pipe without putting your hand down.

Air: Leaving the ground by jumping or leaping ("catching air").

Air to Fakie Spin: An air version of the nollie—a 180 Air that starts riding forward and ends riding fakie.

Alley Oop: A counter-rotated 180 Air.

Alley Oop Mute Grab: A Mute Air mixed with an Alley Oop.

Alpine: Fast, carving freeriding with stiff, sturdy equipment. Also known as free carving.

Alpine Race: Timed, downhill events through changing terrain and around gates. Events include the super G, giant slalom (GS), parallel GS, slalom, and parallel slalom.

Amplitude: An International Snowboard Federation and USSA judging criteria in halfpipe competitions. It represents the volume of execution—the degree of power and energy shown in the ride—and is measured by the competitor's used energy.

Andrecht: Named for Dave Andrecht. A one-handed handplant done on the trailing hand while grabbing the board with the leading hand.

Asymmetrical: A board that shifts or changes the sidecut, flex patterns, or other features from one edge to the other.

Backcountry: Remote, undeveloped areas reachable only by snow cat, helicopter, snowmobile, or hiking in.

Backside: The area behind your back when you're in a halfpipe or doing a trick off a wall. If you're describing the backside wall in a pipe, it's the wall behind you. If you're turning backside during a trick, your back is uphill. The backside wall can also be defined as the left wall for regular foot and the right wall for goofy foot.

Backside Air Grab: Performed by jumping off the backside wall and turning 180 degrees back into the pipe, then grabbing the heel edge near the nose with the front hand.

Bail: On plate bindings, the heavy metal wire that locks hard boots down.

Banked Slalom Race: Resembles a typical slalom race, but the course has steeply banked walls and elevated gates.

Base: The bottom of the snowboard.

Base Preparation: The second tuning step in taking care of a snowboard. Old wax and dirt and are removed, and the base is checked for levelness.

Base Repair: The third tuning step in taking care of a snowboard. Scratches and gouges in the base are filled in, and protrusions are removed.

Base Structuring: The fourth tuning step in taking care of a snowboard. By sanding, brushing, or using a riller bar (a special tool with small teeth), it puts a finely grooved pattern into the base that cuts down on the dragging effects of friction and suction.

Bevel: To file a slight angle into the side edge or base edge when tuning the snowboard's edges.

Binding: The device that locks your boots to the board. Highback bindings are used with soft boots, and plate bindings are used with hard boots.

Blindside: A clockwise rotation for regular riders and a counterclockwise rotation for goofy riders. It's called "blindside" because it's harder to see in that direction.

Blunt Nose Slide: A sideways tip wheelie.

BoarderCross: A race that combines elements of freeriding, racing, and jumping. This is the only event where riders compete head-to-head.

Bone: To fully extend one or both legs.

Bonedrecht: An Andrecht with the back leg boned out.

Bonk: Hitting an object on purpose with the snowboard.

Bunny Hop: In a halfpipe, turning in the air, instead of on the wall.

Caballerial: A trick that starts fakie, spins approximately 360 degrees, and lands in your original stance. The halfpipe version is a 360 Air that starts fakie and ends forward.

Camber: The bridge-like arc in the center of the board that lifts the middle of the board off the snow.

Canadian Bacon: A backside halfpipe trick using the back hand to grab the toe edge while reaching through your legs.

Cant Plate: A beveled plate that tilts your binding and foot up at an angle. It lifts the heel higher than the toes, or vice versa.

Carved Turn: A turn that uses the board's sidecut to slice an arc through the snow.

Center of Mass: An imaginary point between the belly button and tailbone. It helps determine which end of the snowboard travels downhill first.

Chairlift: A series of seats suspended from a cable that transports riders up a mountain. Types include doubles (two-seaters), triples (three-seaters), and quads (four-seaters). The best chair to learn on is a detachable quad chair.

Chicken Salad Grab: A through-the-legs grab to the heel edge with the back hand. The rider bones out the front leg, sits over the tip, and reaches through the legs to grab the heel edge.

Crail Grab: Grabbing the toe edge near the nose with your back hand and boning your back leg.

Crippler: A J-Tear Air without a handplant.

Crud: Powder that has been tracked out, or unpredictable snow.

Crust: Snow that is hard and crusty on the top, but softer underneath.

Deck: The protective top-sheet of the snowboard, where the bindings are mounted.

Detuning: To dull the tip and tail edges of the snowboard beyond the effective edge. Prevents the edges from catching when gliding straight, or from hooking too early at the start of a turn.

Difficulty: A USSA judging criterion in halfpipe competitions. The judges rate the difficulty of a maneuver as well as the way that different maneuvers are put together to form the competitor's unique run.

Duckfoot: A stance that angles the toes of both feet out in opposite directions.

Edge Filing: The first tuning step in taking care of a snowboard. Maintaining sharp edges helps you initiate turns and grip the snow.

Edge: A strip of steel that runs the length of the board on either side of the base.

Eggplant: An Andrecht with the front hand planted instead of the back hand. The front hand is then grabbed with the back hand.

Elguerial: A fakie to forward (or forward to fakie) 360 handplant flip. Named after pro skateboarder Eddie Elguera.

Eurocarve Turn: The opposite of a **Techno-Carve Turn**. The body is laid out over the snow, not balancing over the board, but diving into the turn.

Execution: An International Snowboard Federation judging criterion in halfpipe competitions. It is the fluent style of the jumps executed without fault by the racer.

Extreme Competition: Competitors are flown to the top of a mountain, descend one at a time, and are judged on who performs best in six categories. Riders are judged on aggressiveness/attack, form/technique, fluidity, air, degree of difficulty/line of descent, and control.

Fakie: Riding backward. See also **Switch Stance**.

Falling Leaf: Traversing a zigzag path down a slope.

Fall Line: The path a ball would follow if rolled down a hill; the path of least resistance down any given slope.

50/50 Grind: When the snowboard rides parallel with the rail, traveling straight down it.

Figure-Eight Competition: Two snowboarders are transported to the backcountry, and carve synchronized figure eights down a slope of unmarked powder.

540 Air: A spin-and-a-half that usually starts out forward and ends up fakie. (Also done starting fakie and ending forward.) The halfpipe version starts and ends forward.

Five-O Grind: A wheelie on the rail in the 50/50 position.

Flex: The measure of how soft or hard a board feels when bent along its length.

Freeriding: Plain old riding for fun in any kind of gear.

Freestyle: Doing ground and air tricks, like spins and grabs. Freestyle boards are generally soft and symmetrical.

Fresh Fish Grab: Grab the heel edge with the back hand between the heels, boning out the back leg at the same time. Keep the other arm straight out in the air to counterbalance everything.

Frontside: The area in front of your body. If you're describing the frontside wall in a halfpipe, it's the wall in front of you. A frontside spin is a clockwise spin for goofy riders and a counterclockwise spin for regular riders. The frontside wall can also be defined as the right wall for regular foot and the left wall for goofy foot.

Frontside Air Grab: When leaving the lip, grap the toe edge between the toes with the back hand. Either leg can be boned.

Frontside Invert: A one-handed handstand on the frontside wall.

Garland Turn (garland): A skidded or carved turn in just one direction, each followed by a drop into the fall line. The resulting path looks like a garland draped across a Christmas tree.

Goofy Foot: A snowboarder who rides right-foot forward. Describes both the rider and the stance.

Grab: To grab either edge of the snowboard with one or both hands.

Grind: To slide across an object such as a slider bar or log.

Groomed: Snow that has been manicured by special snow cats or other grooming equipment.

Half-Cab: A fakie to fakie halfpipe trick where the board turns approximately 180 degrees.

Halfpipe: A U-shaped trench with walls on either side designed to help snowboarders accelerate and catch air on both walls.

Halfpipe Competition: An event where riders push the limits of aerial showmanship. Events include music, specialized equipment, and cutting-edge lingo.

Handplant: A halfpipe trick where the rider does a handstand on one or both hands.

Hard Boot: A stiff boot designed to work with plate bindings.

Heel Edge: The edge of the snowboard nearest your heels.

Highback Binding: A binding that uses straps to hold soft boots on a snowboard.

Hybrid Step-In Boot: Soft boots that incorporate step-in binding technology.

Iguana Alley Oop: An Alley Oop done while grabbing the toe edge with the back hand near the tail.

Indy Air Grab: The back hand grabs the toe edge between the toes.

Indy Nose Bone Grab: An Indy Air Grab with the front leg boned out.

Indy Tail Bone Grab: An Indy Air Grab with the back leg boned out.

Indy Tuck Knee Grab: An Indy Air Grab with the back knee dropped to the board.

Insert: A threaded hole in the deck of the board that accepts bolts when the bindings are mounted.

Invert: A trick where the head is beneath the board.

Japan Air Grab: Like the **Mute Air Grab**, but the back is arched and the board is pulled up behind almost to head level.

J-Bar Tow: A hook-shaped bar that rests behind riders and pulls them up the hill.

Jib: Describes a type of riding where snowboarders slide rails, bonk boxes, and contact other obstacles.

Jacoby (J-)Tear: A 540 backflip handplant. Invented by Mike Jacoby.

Jump Turn: Turning the board while airborne.

Landing: A USSA judging criterion in halfpipe competitions. The competitor's balance, precision, stability, and rhythm are analyzed.

Late Spin: Uses the same coil and recoil motion as a shifty. The last half-spin is held back until just before landing, when the board is spun powerfully around to stick the landing.

Layback Air: A one-handed handstand on the frontside wall of a halfpipe.

Layback Slide: Approaching a wall on an uphill edge, the rider leans back toward the tail and kicks the back foot forward (downhill). (With the back facing downhill, this is called a **backside slash**.)

Leash: A strap used to attach the snowboard to your front leg so that it doesn't escape.

Lien Air Grap: Developed by Neil Blender. The rider sits over the nose with the back leg boned, and grabs the heel edge near the tip with the front hand.

Lip: The top edge of a halfpipe (at the top of the wall).

McTwist: A front-flip-540 twist.

Melanchollie Air: A frontside trick using the front hand to grab the heel edge between the bindings.

Method Air Grab: The rider grabs the heel edge between the heels with the front hand and pulls the board up behind to head level.

Miller Flip: A one-handed 180 handstand named after Darrel Miller.

Mute Air Grab: The rider grabs the toe edge with the front hand between the toes or near the tip and bones the back leg for style with the back hand thrown skyward.

900 Air: Two-and-a-half spins in the air.

Nollie: An ollie off the nose (tip). It can be combined with a 180-degree spin to end the trick riding fakie.

Nose: The front, or tip, of the snowboard.

Nose Bone (Poke): Straightening out the front leg.

Nose Roll: A sliding 180 spin off the front of the board.

Nose Slide: Like a rock-n-roll, but the rail is between the front foot and the nose.

Nuclear: A backside trick using the back hand to grab the heel edge near the nose.

Obstacle Course: A timed alpine race with jumps, quarterpipes, and wave sites.

Offset: The measure of how far the center of the desired stance is from the center point of the board's length.

Ollie: A way to attain air on flat ground with or without a jump.

180 Air: The rider starts riding forward, spins 180 degrees in the air and ends up riding fakie.

Palmer Grab: The rider grabs the heel edge between the heels with the front hand and throws the board out to the side.

Plate Binding: A binding that fastens hard boots to the board with sturdy steel bails.

Poma (Platter) Lift: Similar to a T-bar, with a disk on a metal rod that is placed between the legs. Each person rides separately.

P-Tex: Polyethylene used in snowboard bases.

P-Tex candle: A drip-repair candle made of paraffin and polyethylene plastic. Used to repair gouges in snowboard bases.

Quarterpipe: Halfpipe with only one wall.

Rail: The side of a snowboard comprised of the sidewall and edge.

Regular Foot: A snowboarder who rides left-foot forward. Describes both the rider and the stance.

Revert: A late 180 spin on the snow that goes from riding fakie back to riding normal or vice versa.

Roast Beef Grab: A through-the-legs grab to the heel edge with the back hand. The rider bones out the back leg, sits over the tip, and reaches through the legs to grab the heel edge.

Rock-n-Roll Grind: The snowboard is straight across the rail and the rail is halfway between the feet. The tip must be kept up.

Rope Tow: A continuous loop of moving rope that pulls riders up the hill.

Sad Andrecht: An Andrecht with the front leg boned out.

Seatbelt: A backside air using the front hand to grab the toe edge near the tail.

720 Air: Two full spins in the air.

Shifty: In the air, the upper and lower body twist in opposite directions (coil and recoil). The board is spun back under the upper body just before landing.

Shovel: The lifted or upward-curve sections of a snowboard at the tip and tail.

Sidecut: The arc that gives a snowboard a slight hourglass shape. When the board flexes during a turn, the sidecut comes in contact with the hill and helps carve turns.

Sidekick: Trying to kick your butt with your board during a jump.

Sideslip: Skidding downhill on the uphill edge with the board perpendicular across the hill.

Skating: Pushing the snowboard with the back foot on the ground and the front foot in the binding.

Sketching: Skidding outward during a turn or temporarily losing control.

Skidded Turn: A turn that uses foot, leg, and body movements to turn the snowboard instead of relying on the board's sidecut to carve a turn.

Slide Turn: A skidded turn done on the transitions of a halfpipe.

Slob Air Grab: The rider grabs the toe edge near the nose with the front hand and bones the back leg during the grab. A **double-handed Slob** is grabbing with both hands.

Slopestyle: Array of tricks staying close to the ground.

Slopestyle Competition: A freestyle competition that displays riding ability and showmanship and can include quarterpipes, spines, waves, rails, boxes, and logs.

Smith Grind: Like a rock-n-roll, but the tip is lower and more forward than the tail.

Snow Cat: A tractor-powered machine used to groom slopes. Also provides a way for taking snowboarders to otherwise inaccessible terrain.

Snowboard Park: An area that contains slider bars, boxes, rails, halfpipes, quarterpipes, or other natural or man-made obstacles.

Soft Boot: A flexible snowboarding boot for use with highback bindings.

Spaghetti Air: A double-handed Slob variation. The rider reaches the back hand forward through the legs and grabs the toe edge next to the front hand, while sitting over the board and boning the back leg.

Stale Fish Grab: The rider reaches the back arm around the back leg to grab the heelside edge between the bindings.

Stalemasky: A backside trick using the front hand to reaches through the legs to grab the heel edge.

Stance: The position of your feet on the snowboard. The term can include other aspects, like regular or goofy stances, stance width, and foot angles.

Step-in Binding: A strapless, locking binding that provides a more convenient method of engaging the foot to the snowboard. Introduced as an alternative to highback bindings.

Stiffy Grab: The rider grabs the toeside edge between the bindings with either hand. At the peak of the air, both legs are boned straight out.

Stomp Pad: A rubber or soft plastic mat that sticks to the top of the deck between the bindings. It keeps the back foot on the board when the foot isn't locked into the back binding.

Style: A USSA judging criterion in halfpipe competitions. Demonstrated by smooth, powerful riding, and holding grabs, boning, and tweaking. It is increased by accentuating the maneuver, and decreased by falling or flailing.

Switch Stance: To ride the board backward, with the opposite foot forward than you would normally have.

Tail: The back end of the board.

Tail Bone (Poke): Straightening out the back leg.

Tail Grab or Snatch: Using the back hand to grab the tail.

Tail-Grab Alley Oop: An Alley Oop done while grabbing the tail edge with the back hand.

Tail Roll: A sliding 180 spin off the back of the board.

Tail Slide: Like a rock-n-roll, but the rail is between the back foot and the rail.

Tail Wheelie: Leaning way back on the board and pull-ing the tip up off the snow.

Tai-Pan Grab: Reaching through the legs with the front hand and grabbing the toe edge between the toes.

T-Bar Tow: Similar to a J-bar tow, with bars that look like upside-down Ts attached to a moving cable. Designed to pull two people uphill at one time.

Techno-Carve Turn: A smooth, fast, technically precise carved turn where the boarder's hips and shoulders are more perpendicular to the long axis of the board, perfectly balanced over the boards' carving edge.

360 Air: A complete spin in the air. Also called a **360** or a **Helicopter**. A **Fakie to Fakie 360** is performed by starting and ending riding fakie. In the halfpipe version (**Air to Fakie**), the midair turn back into the pipe forces a fakie landing.

Tip: The front, or nose, of the snowboard.

Toe Edge: The edge of the snowboard nearest your toes.

Torsional Stiffness: The measure of how hard it is to twist the board along its length.

Transition (Tranny): The curved section of a halfpipe between the vertical part of the wall and the flat.

Traverse: To ride across a hill or halfpipe.

Tuck: Pulling the knees into the chest during a jump.

Tuning: Keeping the snowboard in good condition. Steps include **Edge Filing**, **Base Preparation**, **Base Repair**, **Base Structuring**, and **Waxing**.

Two-Handed Invert Handplant: A two-handed upside-down handstand in a halfpipe. If the handstand is held for a long time, the trick becomes a **Ho-Ho**.

Unweighting: Lightening the snowboard by rising with your body, pulling up your knees, or letting the board rise off the terrain.

Variety: An International Snowboard Federation and USSA judging criterion in halfpipe competitions. It is the total number of different maneuvers during the run. Four different categories should be represented, consisting of vertical rotation, horizontal rotation, upright jumps, and lip tricks.

Vertical (Vert): The vertical portion of a wall in a halfpipe.

Wall: The transition and vertical parts of a halfpipe combined, forming the wall.

Walt Air: A backside trick using the front hand to grab the heel edge near the tail.

Waxing: The fifth step in tuning a snowboard. Makes it easier for the snowboard to glide over the snow, and protects the base from moisture, UV rays, snow contaminants, and dirt.

Wedge (Bevel) Plate: A plate or foam bevel used in or beneath the bindings to tilt the outside of your foot in toward the arch.

Weighting: Making the snowboard heavier by sinking into it with your body, flexing your knees, and letting the board grab the snow.

Index

145